Early Praise for Adulting Unplugged!

"This book is a must have for all parents to ensure they prepare their teen for adulthood. Traci points out the main areas that parents often overlook before launching their teens into the world beyond their household. She also explains practical ways to work on these skills. Parents will be prepared to make their teen's transition into adulthood a little bit smoother."

Sheri Gazitt, Founder and CEO of Teen Wise

"As the parent of several teenagers and young adults, I wish I had this book when my children were younger. Adulting Unplugged! is an excellent guide to help you and your children navigate life as they prepare for adulthood. There are so many practical ideas and exercises for helping your children approach everything from healthy communication and lifestyles to financial literacy and critical thinking skills."

Amy, Homeschool Mama

Adulting Unplugged

Preparing Your Homeschool Teen for Life After High School

Traci Bakenhaster

This book is dedicated to my mom, who has always been my biggest supporter, encourager, and fiercest defender. You are the strongest woman I know, and your belief in me has helped me push past my limits and past hardships, and driven me to achieve my dreams.

I also want to dedicate this book to my own two children, Conner and Mattie. You are blessings from God, and my inspiration for everything that I do. I'm so grateful that He picked me to be your mom.

CONTENTS

1

LET ME INTRODUCE MYSELF

H i, I'm Traci Bakenhaster, the founder of Adulting University, and the author of this book, *Adulting Unplugged*. I am so glad you are here, and that you have decided to read this book to empower you and your teen!

I have been working with teens and young adults for most of my career, for more than 12 years in fact. I've worked in all kinds of industries, from higher education and career tech to small business to corporations. I have four college degrees, including two associate, a bachelor's, and a master's, and a multitude of certifications (can we say forever nerd?).

For the past 4.5 years, I have been the proprietor of Adulting University, where we empower homeschool moms to transform their family dynamics, unlocking the potential within their teens to become confident, capable, and compassionate adults. We do this through interactive curriculum, parent support, and even our AU Virtual Co-op!

However, before all of this, I was like many young adults. Living life, not a care in the world, no responsibility, no real vision for my future. You see, before I left home, I got married to my high school sweetheart. He was in the military, so right after graduating high school, I moved more than 10 hours away from my family to live off-base. Long story short, it didn't work out, and I ended up moving back home, where I moved in with my grandma.

When I moved back, I wasn't making the best decisions. The good, well-behaved girl in high school who got almost straight A's was lost, insecure, and looking for love and acceptance in the wrong places after being thrown away by the "love of her life." Then one day, everything changed...

It was a rainy spring day as I walked into the windowless bathroom at a friend's house. I opened my bag and pulled out the box inside. Slowly, I read through the directions. I didn't want to mess it up. I needed an accurate result.

It said the results could take 30 seconds, so I slowly paced back and forth under the dim lights. I remember thinking, *This feels like an eternity*. Finally, time was up. I slowly approached the side of the sink, where I had laid the test strip down. I slowly reached down, picked it up, and looked: *Are there two lines? Is that a positive or negative?* Two lines . . . *positive*. I slowly sat down on the toilet seat and smiled. I had never felt peace like this. It was as if time had stopped, and I felt truly happy for the first time.

Not the reaction most 20 years olds would have, especially when you weren't even with the dad. But there I was, happy, excited. I had someone to live for, to love, and pour into who wouldn't leave me like everyone else had.

Fast forward 9 months, and after 20 hours of labor and 2 hours of pushing, there was the most beautiful little boy. He was the absolute best baby, and living with my grandma, he was also the most spoiled.

That was the tipping point. The moment when I decided I was going to do something with my life because that helpless, innocent little munchkin needed me. Not long after he was born, I enrolled in our local community college, and then signed up for government assistance to help with childcare and formula.

I didn't have many bills, especially living with my grandma, and college was free because, as a single parent living beneath the poverty line, I received plenty of grants to pay for school.

I remember the day I graduated with my first associate degree. It didn't feel real. As I walked across the stage, palms sweaty, I was afraid that I was going to trip and fall on my face. I remember my family being there to celebrate with me. I knew I wanted to keep going, so I transferred my credits to The Ohio State University, where I wanted to major in business.

During this time, I decided I really needed to be "on my own." Living with my grandma and her great-grandchild wasn't the best situation. So, I began the search for my own apartment.

I spent hours researching and looking for options that I could afford in a good part of town. Finally, I found one. It was an income-restricted two-bedroom apartment that I easily qualified for because I was making a whopping $17,500 per year in income from my part-time job while enrolled in school full time.

I still spent a lot of time at my grandma's. She and I were very close, and she was my favorite person (well, she and my mom).

One day, my grandma had to go to the hospital for a fairly straightforward procedure. While there, she contracted "hospital pneumonia," which is basically a very difficult strain of pneumonia to treat and get rid of. The doctors said she would be fine and was on the mend.

It was October 16, 2016. I woke up and got ready to take my son to daycare and go to work. I had a few extra minutes, so I sat down on the couch and opened Facebook. One of my distant cousins in another state had tagged me in a post.

As I opened the post, my heart stopped...

"Heaven has gained an angel today. Sending you so much love..." Then I saw my mom's name, those of my uncle and cousins, and then mine.

I didn't understand. There was no way she could be gone. I just saw her last night, not even 12 hours ago! My heart racing, I called my mom, and as soon as I heard her voice, I burst into tears and all that would come out was "What!?"

She told me that my grandma didn't make it . . . that someone was supposed to be there to tell me in person, but they didn't make it in time.

Another pivotal moment in my life.

This was the first time I had ever experienced this type of loss. This type of complete and total devastation. It felt like I lost a part of myself that day. My grandma was my biggest cheerleader, my closest family member, the one I spent days on end with and went shopping with, the one who introduced me to coffee and Beanie Babies and Clown Cone Ice Cream. She wasn't supposed to go yet. She was supposed to be there to see me graduate with my bachelor's degree, to see my son grow up...

After I lost my grandma, I needed time to process. I quit my job at the college, and a few months later started a new job with a small bump in pay. After the new year, I decided

I was tired of paying rent and that it was a waste of money. So, I looked into buying my first house.

After several months, I finally found the perfect home. It had character; it was a fixer upper (which I love!), and with my down payment, it was less money each month than my rent! I wanted my son to have space, a yard, a place to call home.

That's when life really started. When the real meaning of "adulting" became reality.

It started less than a month after moving in. It was time to renew my government benefits, just like every year. However, this would be my first time renewing with my new job. I thought nothing of it. I mean, after all, $23,000 a year was nothing!

I was wrong . . . *so very wrong*.

"You're no longer eligible for assistance due to your income. You exceed the monthly limit for a household of two by $50 a month," the paper read. I stood there stunned. Immediately, I called customer service, completely panicked. It had to be a mistake. There was no way I was making too much money! My income of $23,000 could barely cover our living expenses, let alone childcare and food costs.

I will never forget what the lady said to me . . . "I'm so sorry. Unfortunately, you exceed the poverty line eligibility requirements. They are set in stone. Even if you made ONE CENT over, you would lose eligibility."

And just like that, I now had expenses that easily exceeded my income. There was no gradual decline, no prorated benefits, just a straight cutoff. Now mind you, I had never planned on making these benefits a long-term thing. It was just to help me stay on my feet until I got my degree and acquired a good-paying full-time job. But the government had other plans.

So, there I was, $650 per month for my mortgage, $250 per month for my car, and now from $0 to $400 per month in groceries and food, and from $20 per week to $195 per week for childcare. You can probably see that the math isn't quite *mathing*...

I knew nothing about money outside of a basic finance class I took at the community college, which I didn't really find all too relevant. And now, I had expenses that were well outside what I could afford. So what did I do? What any sane single parent would do, of course . . . I picked up a second job. That still wasn't quite enough, so then I picked up a third.

That still couldn't quite cover it. I wasn't managing my money, as I didn't know how. I didn't have a budget and didn't even know what a budget was. I was living off student loans, credit cards, and even a home equity loan.

I made some very poor decisions with money during this time.

Things changed when I went to a financial planner friend who told me about Dave Ramsey. My friend shared how to budget and helped me create a plan to get out of debt. But if I'm being honest, things didn't really change and start getting better until I got a full-time job more than a year later.

During this time, I also had a slew of other things go wrong that cost a pretty penny. The worst was when the main sewage line in my backyard collapsed, and of course the home warranty wouldn't do a thing about it. So there was another more than $3,000 fix...

Now, mind you, I was still going to school full time, working three jobs, and taking care of a toddler. It was a very tough season, and frankly, I don't really remember much of it.

What I do remember is the first time I met my husband at job number 2. The most awkward conversation ensued at the printer, in a deathly quiet stereotypical office. I'm sorry for anyone who witnessed that because it had to be very uncomfortable. After that, we didn't speak to each other again until it was his last day before starting a new job. And the rest is history.

It is amazing when you look at how God works. My husband and I started dating a little more than a month before I graduated with my bachelor's degree. I was so sad that my grandma couldn't be at the graduation, but my husband was, and he celebrated with me and my family. And he's been there ever since.

There have been plenty of challenges and hardships along the way (that's a book for another time). But what I learned is that I wasn't prepared for life. I had to struggle and push through and figure so many things out on my own because my family couldn't help me. Not because they didn't want to, but because they didn't know how.

No one taught me about healthy relationships or about how to manage my emotions, which always got the best of me. I didn't know how to have healthy boundaries, stand up for myself, or manage money.

That's why I created this book. To help moms who love their children and want the best for them, who don't want life to knock them down, or fail to reach their full potential because of costly mistakes. This book is your guide to helping you prepare your teens for life after high school.

Here is the reality. We as parents want the best for our kids. We want them to grow up to be successful, to have great jobs and great relationships, to be happy and fulfilled. We want our kids to have everything that we couldn't or didn't have, and yet so often, just like my parents, we have all the best intentions, but we fall short on the most important things in life. And then instead of smooth sailing, we see our kids going down the same path we did, riding the struggle bus of life.

BUT...

You are here reading this book. You are changing your family for the better, and you are pouring into yourself and into your teen so that you can be the best version of yourself and to help your teen be the best version of themselves.

Together, we are going to make that struggle bus of life a lot smoother, and equip you and your teen with the essential skills they will need no matter where they go in life.

I'm not guaranteeing perfection, but what I am guaranteeing is that if you take the principles you learn in this book and actually apply them to your life and your teen's life, you will see an improvement in the preparedness of your teen for the real world.

Each chapter of this book will dive into a specific topic to help you help your teen be the best version of themselves, and be successful in life. We're covering foundational skills that every teen needs to know, like communication, emotional intelligence, financial literacy, and even independent living.

Each chapter provides real-world examples, tips and tricks, and activities you can do with your teen to improve in that area! There are so many goodies in this book that I suggest being ready to take notes on any aha moments you may have along the way!

In fact, the best way to get the most out of this book is to take the time to implement what you have learned. To do that, I suggest you focus on one chapter at a time.

Alright mama, are you ready to get started? LET'S GO!!

RESULT:
A capable, confident, and independent young adults who can navigate life's challenges with ease instead of feeling lost and unprepared.

INTERPERSONAL & COMMUNICATION SKILLS	CRITICAL THINKING & INDEPENDENCE	HEALTH, SAFETY & DIGITAL WELLNESS	PERSONAL RESPONSIBILITY & SELF-DISCIPLINE
ASSERTIVENESS & ADVOCACY	THINKING FOR YOURSELF & AVOIDING BAD ADVICE	KEEPING SAFE IN THE REAL WORLD	HANDLING FAILURE & BUILDING RESILIENCE
WORKPLACE & PROFESSIONAL COMMUNICAT.	CAREER EXPLORATION & READINESS	PHYSICAL WELLNESS & PERSONAL CARE	HOUSEHOLD & LIFE RESPONSIBILITY
PERSONAL RESPONSIBILITY & SELF-DISCIPLINE	FINANCIAL LITERACY & MONEY MANAGEMENT	DIGITAL WELLNESS & SOCIAL MEDIA SAFETY	DEVELOPING GRIT, MOTIVATION & WORK ETHIC
CONFLICT RESOLUTION & EMOTIONAL INTELLIGENCE	DECISION-MAKING & PROBLEM-SOLVING	MANAGING STRESS & MENTAL HEALTH	TIME MANAGEMENT & ORGANIZATION

ADULTING UNIVERSITY VIRTUAL CO-OP

2

REALITY CHECK

L et's get real for a second. You've probably heard this: "Kids these days just aren't ready for the real world." And while we may roll our eyes at this cliché, there is some truth to it. Today's teens—our future generation of adults—are entering a world that is more complex, competitive, and fast paced than ever before. But here's the kicker: They're alarmingly unprepared to handle it.

If you're a homeschool parent, you're already ahead of the curve. You care deeply about your teen's education and personal development, but there's something more happening here. We're not just talking about whether your teen can pass a test or score well on the SATs—we're talking about whether they can thrive in the real world. And the data isn't looking good.

The Workplace Is Sounding the Alarm

Startling statistics paint a clear picture of what's happening. A survey by Education Week reports that only 28% of employers feel confident that Gen Z is ready for the workforce.

Employers have voiced growing concerns that today's young adults are missing key skills like effective communication, time management, and even basic professionalism. This isn't a minor gap—it's a chasm.

A separate survey published by Newsweek Incorporated goes deeper, revealing that 40% of employers feel that Gen Z lacks essential job readiness skills. Skills like problem solving, emotional regulation, and critical thinking—the very things that help a person thrive in a career—are all areas where our teens are falling short. When it comes to collaborating, working independently, or managing deadlines, many teens are simply not prepared to navigate these essential aspects of the workplace.

Employers are also facing a challenge that's new to this generation: digital dependency. While Gen Z is the most digitally connected generation, many employers note that this reliance on technology can be a double-edged sword. Sure, they know how to use apps, tools, and platforms, but with in-person communication or complex problem solving without the aid of a search engine, Gen Z struggles.

The Johns Hopkins Imagine Center also highlights how modern workplaces are finding it difficult to adapt to a workforce that's not only lacking soft skills but also often suffers from heightened levels of anxiety and emotional unpreparedness in professional settings. Employers are asking for resilience and initiative, but Gen Z is entering the workforce already overwhelmed.

Parents Are Feeling the Pressure Too

Parents are feeling the weight of this as well. According to a Gallup poll, over 60% of parents avoid having difficult but necessary conversations with their teens about critical life skills like budgeting, mental health, or even basic household management. The reason? Many parents either feel they're not equipped to have these conversations or are unsure how to approach them. They're afraid of creating tension or overwhelming their teen, and sometimes they're simply too busy to focus on these essential yet often uncomfortable lessons.

A survey from Pew Research found that over 70% of parents worry their teens aren't ready for the responsibilities of adulthood. The problem is, while we as parents want our teens to be self-sufficient, we rarely know how to teach them the skills they'll need in the real world. And if we don't know where to start, how can we expect our teens to be prepared?

Parents are facing a unique dilemma: To protect their kids from stress or failure, they sometimes shelter them from the very challenges that would help them grow. And while technology has made many aspects of life easier, it has also isolated teens from hands-on, real-world experiences. The Parent Today report points out that teens today are less likely to take on traditional responsibilities like part-time jobs, household chores, or even driving compared to previous generations. As a result, they're entering adulthood without the confidence or skills to navigate independence.

Teens Aren't Ready for Adulthood

Here's the heart of the issue: Teens themselves know they're not ready. In a poll conducted by UPI, teens admitted they didn't feel equipped to handle basic life skills. Only 24% of teens surveyed said they felt prepared to manage their own finances, whereas a staggering number expressed anxiety about moving into adulthood without the tools to succeed.

And it's not just finances. Whether it's managing stress, cooking a meal, or navigating interpersonal relationships, today's teens are feeling the weight of expectations without the confidence to meet them. Many of them rely heavily on their parents or the Internet to solve problems instead of developing the critical thinking skills they'll need to make decisions on their own.

According to the Education Week survey, 53% of teens struggle with making eye contact during job interviews, and even more struggle with basic communication skills. The shift from in-person communication to digital conversations is leaving teens anxious and unsure of how to navigate real-world, face-to-face interactions.

Why This Book? Why Now?

So, what does all this mean for you and your teen? It means that although the statistics may seem bleak, they present an opportunity. This book, *Adulting Unplugged*, is your guide to stepping in where traditional education and modern technology have fallen short. It's designed specifically for homeschool parents like you, who understand that preparing your teen for adulthood goes far beyond academics.

In this book, we'll cover the life skills that matter most—skills that will help your teen communicate effectively, manage their emotions, build healthy relationships, and take control of their financial future. We'll break down the essentials of emotional intelligence, critical thinking, digital safety, and much more.

This isn't about preparing your teen for the next test—it's about preparing your teen for life.

Grab our workbook to make the most out of your book.

ADULTING
UNIVERSITY

ESTABLISHED 2022

3

TALKING THE TALK

TEACHING YOUR TEEN EFFECTIVE COMMUNICATION

"**S**top arguing with me." "Lose the attitude." "How many times have I told you to *not* do that?" Sound familiar? These are statements we have heard A LOT in our house over the past few years. Oftentimes as parents, when it comes to talking to our preteens or teenagers, we feel like a broken record, or like we are talking to a wall. Sometimes our conversations end in arguments, with someone feeling unheard, misunderstood, frustrated, or just disconnected.

And let me tell you, even as someone who teaches this stuff, I am not immune to the "broken record syndrome." In fact, my son has ADHD and is like the Energizer Bunny, on steroids, with the attention span of a rabbit. I love him to death, of course, AND he drives me and my husband absolutely bonkers sometimes!

However, the main issue that this chapter is going to cover is not just getting your teen to listen to you—it's deeper than that. This chapter is going to help you connect with your teen, to create a connection and a place that gets you and your teen on the same page.

Communicating with your teenager can feel like navigating a maze or speaking a foreign language. As they enter their teen years, the once clear and open lines of communication can become strained and challenging. This chapter dives deep into a topic that's near and dear to every parent's heart: communicating with their teenagers. In this crazy journey of parenting, having open and honest lines of communication with our teens can be a rewarding yet huge challenge.

But first, let's talk about this challenge you are facing with your teen...

The Teen Communication Challenge

As parents, we often experience a disconnect when our children hit their teenage years. It's like they start speaking an entirely different language. The teen years are hard enough on their own, and trying to communicate with our children can make us feel frustrated, annoyed, or even defeated, like we are never going to get through to them again.

So what ends up happening when you and your teen aren't speaking the same language? What happens when you're not on the same page? For one thing, the misunderstandings may lead to conflicts or the teen resenting you. Those conflicts can create tension in your home. And then the emotional piece comes into play. It's like having a toddler in their terrible twos all over again! The screaming, shouting, crying...it's a mess! If this type of disconnect continues, and the anxiety and stress keep going up, eventually your teen is going to feel undervalued or misunderstood. Then so long to them coming to you to talk anymore.

In their minds, *why talk to mom and dad if all they're going to do is argue, tell me I'm wrong, make me the bad guy, lecture me, or get me into trouble?*

Here's the reality...

Teens are navigating a whirlwind of hormonal, social, and emotional changes. Their brains are still developing, particularly the areas responsible for decision making and impulse control. Meaning, just because they think they're grown up, their brain actually isn't—they just don't know that yet! Have you ever tried to argue with a know-it-all? Someone who is dead set in their ways and will not listen to any reason or wisdom? Yeah, that's what it's like trying to communicate with a teenager who is going through puberty...

Understanding these changes is crucial for parents aiming to maintain open lines of communication. This helps us change our thinking about why our kids are suddenly acting out, or giving "tude," or overall just more feisty or emotional. They aren't doing it on purpose. Their body is just having a complete meltdown, and they don't know how to handle it or what to do. We're all moms, right? So think of having PMS, but instead of just 1 week a month, it lasts from like 12 to 18!

So, you might be wondering... "Hmmm . . . okay. So this might explain WHY my teen is acting like this, and why communicating has become so hard, but WHAT can I do to improve our communication when they're experiencing things out of their control?"

At Adulting University, everything we do we put into what we call our *foundational pillars*, and then each of those pillars is made up of blocks. These blocks are core pieces that you have to have completely full to have a nice solid pillar. When it comes to communication, our belief is that the four foundational pillars are Communication Styles, Relationships, Conflict Resolution, and Speaking.

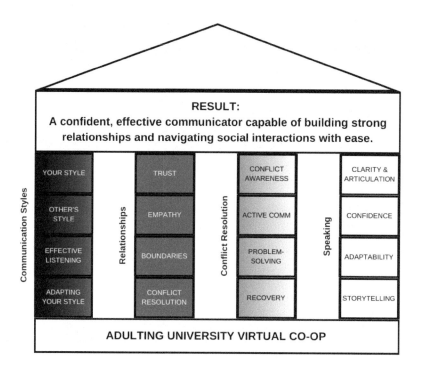

Now, since we only have a chapter, and not an entire book, to teach you all the things about communication, we are going to focus on the first two blocks of our second pillar, which is Relationships.

Next, we are going to dive deeper into the two blocks of the Relationships pillar, which are Trust Building and Empathy. These are foundational to everything else you learn in this book, because if you can have healthy communication with your teenager, then it will make teaching all these other skills SO MUCH easier!

Block #1: Trust Building

"I HATE YOU!!" Have you ever heard those words from your teen? Those horrible words that take a knife to your heart. Words you never thought the precious child you birthed would ever say to you. And if you haven't heard them yet, well, I hate to be the bearer of bad news, but, yeah, it is probably coming at some point. And if not, then kudos to you and celebrate that you didn't have to experience the sound of those words to your face (but more likely behind your back . . . sorry).

When our teens become upset with us, they say mean, hurtful things, because more times than not, they are hurting and they don't know how to process their emotions, or are angry for a reason they don't fully understand. (Don't worry, we are covering the emotional management piece in the next chapter.)

Your first step in communicating with your teen is to build trust. Because something happens when we become teenagers—suddenly, our parents are no longer cool, and our friends are legit better than sliced bread, and we pour our hearts and souls to them, and look for advice from our peers instead of the people who raised us!? I know, mind blowing isn't it!?

This is when our teens pull away, and this is when we have to *pull in*, but not in an annoying, in-their-business kind of way. We have to pull in to rebuild that trust with this person who is no longer our innocent kid but now a teen on their way to adulthood. Here are two ways you can build trust with your teen as they enter this new phase of life.

Prioritize Time Together and Be Present

In today's busy world, finding time to connect with your teen can be challenging. Prioritize shared family time, such as having dinner together two to three nights a week. This doesn't have to be elaborate—just sitting down together can make a significant difference. Studies show that regular family meals contribute to better communication, academic performance, and emotional well-being in teens. Growing up, my family had dinner together every single night, and it was a time to have conversations about school and life. Making time for your kids is crucial.

When you show up, it shows your teen that they matter. Show up at their activities and be present in their lives. This doesn't mean being a "helicopter mom," but being available and attentive when needed. Attend events and extracurricular activities, and be there during important moments.

Your presence shows that you value their interests and are supportive—both of which build trust with your teen. I remember as a kid my mom came to EVERYTHING, and I loved it! And because she had done it my whole life, it didn't embarrass me that she was around. She also was very respectful of my space at events, which made me even more comfortable with her being there. I now do this for my son, and will for our daughter too, and even as a preteen, he loves when I come to stuff because he knows I'm there to support him.

Listen to Learn

Who loves it when you are talking to someone and trying to share something important, or vent, or whatever, and the person you're talking to keeps interrupting, or giving their opinion or unsolicited advice? Yeah, my guess is that you probably don't love that approach, and neither does your teen!

Approach conversations with the mindset of learning from your teen rather than lecturing them. This helps create a nonjudgmental environment where they feel heard and understood. When teens feel their parents are genuinely interested in their thoughts and feelings, they are more likely to open up. Active listening and being present are key.

Sometimes my son wants to talk late at night when I'm ready to decompress, but I've learned to catch myself and make the effort to listen. And believe me, bedtime is the last place I want to have a heart-to-heart, but that is the time when *he* feels comfortable and wants to talk to just me. Is it that, or is he just stalling at bedtime? Either way, I cherish those open, honest, and often deep or funny conversations!

These moments are crucial in building trust and maintaining open communication. In the next block, we are going to take the trust building to the next level by talking about how you can better relate to your teen, and how you can make sure they feel heard and understood.

Block #2: Give Empathy

As you repair or build even stronger trust with your teen, the next piece is empathy—that thing we all hear but often confuse with pity or sympathy. To sympathize with someone means you can see that someone is feeling a certain way and feel sorry for them. EMPATHY is stronger—it's more about *feeling their feels* with them. It is stepping into their situation, their emotions, and truly understanding and relating to what they are experiencing in that moment.

As parents, it is CRUCIAL that we have empathy with our children, not just sympathy. Sympathy is just the pat on the back, where empathy is the hug and unconditional love. And here's the thing: empathy doesn't always come naturally, especially with our kids. Especially when we feel they are overreacting or we see a simple solution to the problem at hand. This is when we actually can make or break a relationship with our teen, especially with them communicating to us. If they don't feel like we care, or aren't taking their situation or emotions seriously, then they will shut down and feel they can't rely on you anymore.

And I know, as a mom, you definitely do not want that to happen! So, here are two foundational things you can do to show empathy to your teenager so that they feel heard and feel valued!

Be Mindful of Body Language and Tone

I want you to think about a time where you felt disrespected, not important enough, or maybe insignificant. Now, think about how that person made you feel that way. Was it something they said? How they said it? Or maybe how they felt cold, closed-off, or distant? So many times, the unspoken words impact us just as much, if not more. We've all heard the saying "actions speak louder than words," and it is especially true when it comes to communicating with your teen.

If I told you "You are doing an amazing job as a parent" in a sarcastic tone with a snicker on my face while simultaneously rolling my eyes, how would you take that "compliment"? My guess, probably not very well. The tone of our voice and the body language we put off to our teens impacts how they will take what you are saying.

Your body language and tone of voice play a significant role in communication. Ensure your tone is welcoming and your body language is open. A simple technique is to keep your palms up during conversations to signal openness. Avoid crossing your arms or displaying closed-off body language, which can make teens feel judged or dismissed. When my son comes to talk to me and I'm busy, I've had to remind myself to put down the phone, turn off the TV, and give him my full attention. Being fully present in the moment shows him that I value him and that I care about what he has to say.

You might ask, what does this have to do with empathy? Well, our body language and tone of voice have a powerful presence. When we lean in closer to provide a safe and open space for our teens, when we give them our undivided attention, and when we speak in a sincere, loving, and supportive tone, we are being *intentional* in demonstrating empathy. Now that we know how to approach our teen to show empathy, let's now look at what to say.

Approach Like a Coach

Body language and tone are half of the empathy equation. The other half is what comes out of our mouths. Think back to a time where you were dealing with something tough, lost a loved one, were having a hard time at work, or were fighting with your spouse or best friend. When you were going through something and just needed to talk, who made you feel heard? Who understood what you were dealing with? Who empathized with you? Who felt your feelings, was present with you, cried with you? Who asked questions that made you feel like they cared and not judged?

Now, think about the people you would likely not go to in those situations. If I had to guess, it would probably be a person who likes to lecture or says things like "I told you so…" or "Suck it up, Buttercup. Pull up them big girl pants and move on!" When we are going through something, we want to talk to people who can relate, who can listen, and who will show empathy and support, not judgment, sympathy, or annoyance.

One way you can do this is what we talked about before. Listen to learn. Let them share everything in their heart first. Then, once they have shared, and it is now an appropriate time for you to speak, do one of two things: give statements that show empathy or ask open-ended questions.

When I talk about statements, what I mean is statements that let your teen know you understand, that you hear them, and that you know this is serious to them (even if you think it shouldn't be). Here are some examples of empathetic statements:

- "So if I heard you correctly, you [reiterate what they said]."

- "I am so sorry you are going through this. It must be very difficult for you."

- "I went through something similar to this too, and it made me feel [feelings]. I could only imagine how you are feeling [insert feelings to validate]."

- "I hear how hard this is for you."

Remember, when making these statements, keep it about them. Sometimes we unintentionally make it about us, but try not to do that. Instead, keep the focus on them and their emotions. Now, let's look at a second approach we can do in combination with the preceding statements: ask open-ended questions.

Asking open-ended questions makes coaches so powerful in the transformations we see every day with clients. We ask questions that will encourage the giving of more information, that will help the client put their feelings into words, and often will help them actually come to their own solutions with little to no advice from us. It really is a powerful thing!

By asking open-ended questions, you allow and encourage your teen to share more without you having to say much at all. Here are some great questions that show empathy and that you want to know more about how they feel and be in the moment with them:

- "What happened next?"

- "Can you tell me more about that?"

- "How did that make you feel at that moment?"

- "What do you think would be a good solution?"

- "What do you think are some next steps you could take?"

- "So why do you think you reacted that way?"

- "What do you think you need right now?"

- "What do you need from me right now?"

It is important to note, however, that your tone is VERY important when you make empathetic statements or ask open-ended questions. If you have the wrong tone, your teen will either shut down or say something like "I don't want to talk about it" or

"Stop talking!" Your tone needs to be one of curiosity and love. Keep your voice lower, consistent, and calm, but have a loving tone. Try to avoid a tone that has any judgment in it or sarcasm or any negative emotions, and try not to get too heightened or emotional, as that could escalate the situation.

Remember, with empathy, you have to start with building trust, then empathy comes next. I would suggest that if you don't have the best communication with your teen right now and maybe they get a little triggered when being asked questions, just show support, encouragement, and that you understand what they are experiencing through statements. Eventually, you will slowly add questions into your conversations to go deeper and have more open conversations!

Conclusion

Maintaining open and healthy communication with your teen can be challenging, but it is crucial for their development and your relationship. By building trust and giving empathy, you can foster a stronger connection with your teen. Remember, the goal is to stay connected through the chaos and conflict, guiding your teen through these transformative years.

In the next chapter, we are going to dive into the topic of emotional intelligence to help your teen become more self-aware, which will help them mature into the young man or woman you've dreamed of them becoming!

Put It Into Practice

Here are some activities that you can do with your teen to practice the things we discussed in this chapter and help you be on your way to having a great relationship with your teen!

1. JOINT ACTIVITY: Cook a Meal Together

Cook a meal together, and use this time to talk with your teen using open-ended questions. Remember, stay curious with a happy, supportive tone!

2. SEPARATE ACTIVITY: Write a Note

Write a note to your teen acknowledging something they've been dealing with lately. Let them know you see them and their emotions. Give them some positive statements to encourage them and show you care.

3. TOGETHER EXERCISE: Plan Shared Time

Set a new boundary where you plan a tech-free evening once a week to play games, talk, or simply enjoy each other's company!

4. ROLE-PLAY: Explore Navigating Conflict

Do some role-play exercises with your teen where you go through some imaginary scenarios to practice navigating conflict together and how to identify triggers, de-escalate, and then come to a mutual solution!

Did you grab the workbook yet? If not grab it now!

4

FEELINGS FIRST

NAVIGATING EMOTIONAL SMARTS WITH YOUR TEEN

I f you have kids, which I would imagine you do since you are reading this book, think back to the "terrible twos." A mother's favorite time of life, where we have a snotty-nosed tyrant wreaking havoc on our sanity. That little bundle of joy we brought into the world just a few short years ago is turning our hair gray, giving us wrinkles, and questioning our ability to be a parent. The moment that stage seems behind you, you hit the preteen and teen years and feel like you are back to raising a toddler who has the emotional regulation of a spoon.

Imagine a world where your teen can navigate life's ups and downs with grace, understand their own emotions, and build meaningful relationships.

Sounds great, right? And you might also say "But Traci, how is that even possible?" as you look at your semigrown "child" having a tantrum because you said she couldn't go to her friend's house. Or in my case, our son who had a complete meltdown because he had to play a recorder at his co-op. I'm talking tears on his dinner plate, a full meltdown...

Well, it is all about teaching your teen how to grow their emotional intelligence and ability to regulate, and in this chapter, we are laying the foundation of how to do it. As a homeschooler, you have the unique opportunity to shape your teen's emotional landscape, teaching them to recognize and manage their emotions, develop empathy, and build resilience. Emotional intelligence is the foundation of a well-rounded, successful life, and this chapter is your roadmap to guiding your teen through this vital journey.

We're going to explore the two foundational blocks to developing emotional intelligence with your teen, but first, let's dive a little deeper into what emotional intelligence actually is, and where your teen currently is.

Emotional Intelligence and Your Teen

Okay, quick check-in, are you still with me? Or did I lose you at emotional intelligence? It's okay if I did. Hopefully, in this section, I can show you exactly what emotional intelligence is and how it is currently affecting your teen. Emotional intelligence involves recognizing, understanding, and managing our own emotions, as well as recognizing, understanding, and influencing the emotions of others.

Emotional intelligence means you have understanding of your emotions. You know your triggers. You know why you feel or react the way you do, and then you know how to better address those feelings or reactions. It also means that you can see and recognize these things in others, and be able to, well, get what you want from others in the best way possible.

For teens, developing emotional intelligence is vital for personal and social success. It helps them handle stress, make thoughtful decisions, and build meaningful relationships. Emotional intelligence takes them from being the 2 year old having a complete fit to being the mature adult who can not only process the emotions they're experiencing but also can articulate them and react in a socially acceptable way.

I like to think of King Solomon in the Bible, labeled the wisest man who ever lived. He understood himself and others, and had wisdom that left a ripple effect on generations. I believe that what he truly had was high emotional intelligence. And this is what we want for our teens, right? We want them to know how to manage and process their emotions to make good decisions, have healthy relationships, and be happy and successful.

Now here is the reality: Our teen's brain will not fully develop until they are about 25 years old. This is just a fact. There is nothing we can do about biology, but we can give them the knowledge and tools to help them develop and process things while they are still growing.

To develop emotional intelligence in your teen, we have created a model made up of four foundational blocks. These blocks, if used to their full potential, will automatically improve one's emotional intelligence and abilities. They are Self-Awareness, Self-Regulation, Empathy, and Social Skills. In the next section, we are going to dive deeper into our first and second blocks to lay the foundation for you and your teen.

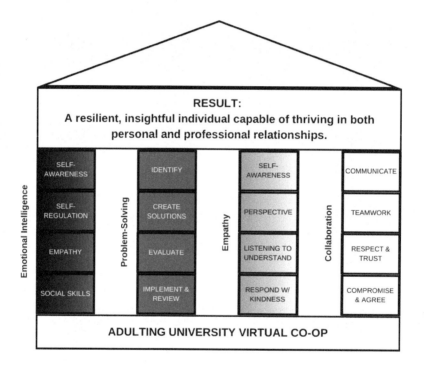

Block #1: Self-Awareness

Have you ever been embarrassed in front of a crowd? I remember the first time I was truly embarrassed and humiliated in front of a group of people. I was in 7th grade, and a group of us and my current "crush" were in our health teacher's classroom during an open period. One girl there was a year older than me and was a bit of a bully. I was wearing my sweatpants that we wore for our basketball games (you might imagine where this is going), and she decided it would be funny to "depants" me in front of the whole room.

There I was, standing with my red sweatpants around my ankles and my pink and purple SpongeBob SquarePants underwear on full display for the entire room to see. I just remember in that moment being so aware of everything going on around me, my heart beating out of my chest, and my face turning as red as a tomato and as hot as an ember. I remember the slow motion of the students all turning toward me and laughing. I remember the posters hanging on the walls, the way the desks were aligned . . . that day will be etched in my brain forever.

During those very short agonizing moments, I had full self-awareness of everything that was going on. And when we talk about being self-aware in the aspect of emotional intelligence, it is like that but with our internal selves. Where we notice all our emotions, thoughts, triggers, feelings, and beyond. Like the movie *Inside Out*, we get to know each individual emotion we have and understand what drives it.

This is the first step to emotional intelligence. To know how to process your emotions and understand others, you have to first be aware of who you are, what you think, how you think, and the why behind it all.

How can you help your teen become more self-aware? Well, there are a couple of things you can do.

Encourage Emotional Vocabulary

Help your teen expand their emotional vocabulary by teaching them words to describe their feelings. We have to be able to describe what we are feeling if we want to understand it. So having your teens expand their vocab from words like bad, good, and okay to words like frustrated, annoyed, angry, hopeless, and overwhelmed will help them start to truly understand what they are feeling. This can then open the door for them to dive deeper into why they feel that way.

For example, if they say they feel "bad," ask for more detail so you can follow up. Are you feeling bad because you are sick? Angry? Annoyed? If you can get to these words first, then you have a better direction in which to go. If they are annoyed, then we can encourage them to ask themselves questions like this: "Who am I annoyed with?" "Why am I annoyed with them?" "What did they do to annoy me?" "How can I process this feeling to not feel annoyed?"

You see, this simple technique of being able to better describe our emotions and feelings opens the door to better understand how we got to this feeling, why we feel this way, and even how to not feel this way in future situations.

So, how can you help your teen expand their vocabulary? Well, by going through our next step of self-awareness...

Do Regular Check-Ins

Did you know that a pilot is always communicating and checking in with his co-pilot? The pilots interact with one another and check in constantly to make sure the other is still in a good place to fly the plane. They will call out if they notice something, because hundreds of lives depend on it. They have to be in sync with one another to make sure the plane gets where it is going safely.

A lot like pilots, we aren't always the main driver in our teen's flight to adulthood, but we can always be the co-pilot, periodically checking in, helping them check in with their emotions, calling out when they seem off, and even checking in by sharing where we are and what we are feeling.

A simple yet powerful way to help your teen become more aware of their emotions and to use better words to describe what they are thinking and feeling is to encourage your teen to check in with their emotions. Ask them questions like "How are you feeling right now?" or "What made you feel that way?" "Why do you think that [situation] bothered you so much?" Simply asking open-ended questions in a nonjudgmental but supportive way can help your teen process their emotions and be aware of what is going on "upstairs."

For some teens, a great way to help them do check-ins with themselves is through journaling. Have your teen consider keeping a daily journal where they track their feelings and what triggered them. This helps in identifying patterns and understanding their emotional responses. If they are a "talk it out" kind of person, have them record themselves talking through their emotions and frustrations and then have them revisit the recording in a few days to have a fresh perspective on what they were experiencing. Once we build a better vocab, and become more aware of the emotions we are feeling, we are then ready to dive a little deeper into the "why."

The 5 Whys

One of my absolute favorite tools that I use with my kids, my clients, and even with parents is this thing called the *5 Whys*. I'm going to quote one of my favorite movies as a teen, *Shrek*: "Ogres are like onions." So are humans. It is never just surface deep. There are multiple layers that we have to go through to get to the truth or root emotion. We are complicated emotional beings. We were created that way. Humans feel some of the most complicated emotions and feelings that no other creature on Earth can. Our teens aren't any different. If anything, the way they experience feelings and emotions is probably even more complex than adults. That is why we sometimes have to peel the layers back one at a time.

Insert the 5 Whys! Think of each "why" being a layer on the onion that is your teenager. When they are talking about their emotions or how they feel about something, practice this exercise. Here is an example:

A teen is working on a math problem and is exhibiting some emotions. You, the homeschool mama, ask, "What is wrong?"

Teen: "Ugh, I am so frustrated right now!"

You: "**Why** do you feel frustrated?"

Teen: "Because I am just not getting it."

You: "**Why** aren't you getting it?"

Teen: "I don't know. I just don't understand it."

You: "**Why** don't you understand it?"

Teen: "I just don't!"

You: "**Why** do you think not understanding it is making you feel frustrated?"

Teen: "I don't know. [pause] Maybe it is because it is making me feel stupid."

You: "**Why** does it make you feel stupid?"

Teen: "Well, because I should be able to do this. Other kids get it and don't struggle like I do."

Because of the 5 Whys Method, we can now identify that in this situation our teen is feeling frustrated, not because they don't understand the math problem, but because they feel inferior to their peers and like they don't measure up. If we would have stopped at the first or second "why," we wouldn't have gotten to the real reason for the emotion that was happening. Now, because we went deeper, we can have a conversation with our teen to help them understand and process what the cause of the actual emotion is so they can recognize their feelings when something like this happens again!

Self-awareness is one of the most valuable skills to have in our toolbox as an adult. It helps us understand our inner voice, values, and what we value most, and what bothers us or hurts us most. We can't have increased emotional intelligence if we don't even understand our emotions to begin with. In our next block, we are going to explore the next step to emotional intelligence, where we can put our awareness into action.

Block #2: Self-Regulation

Our second block to increasing our teen's emotional intelligence is through what is called *self-regulation*. This is the ability to manage and control one's emotions, impulses, and reactions in a variety of settings and situations. I am going to be real with you for a minute, and you may not love what I am about to say, but we as parents have to address these things for our kids' sake. Sometimes, as parents, we have to face realities that we really don't want to. We'd rather live in a bubble than face the hard truth. Well, not today! You are reading the *Adulting Unplugged* book where we have real talk, wrapped in love, because we want you and your teen to succeed in life after high school!

We have all heard the terms thrown out about the younger generations, such as they are *snowflakes*, *fragile*, and *delicate*. These words are harsh, but there is a lot of truth to them. I've worked with teens and young adults for many years, and I can tell you that the majority are not prepared or equipped to handle the harsh realities the world holds. They are not only unaware of their emotions, but they also have no idea how to regulate their emotions, thoughts, and feelings in a way that helps them succeed.

I've seen teens completely fall apart over an emoji in a text message or a post on Instagram. A huge percentage of teens are in counseling for anxiety, depression, and suicidal thoughts that often stem from friend or relationship drama. If they don't learn how to navigate through these emotions and thoughts, teens can internalize these feelings and develop a victim mentality. Now, let me explain before you get too mad and shut the book, and never pick it up again.

Here is why I don't want your teen to be a victim, and why you shouldn't either.

When we become the victim to others and to our own emotions, we give away our power. We give our power to be strong, capable, and emotionally regulated individuals to people who want to tear us down, bulldoze us, or hurt us. And I don't know about you, but I don't want my kids giving their power to ANYBODY. I want them to be equipped with the tools and knowledge to not be a victim, but to stand in their power and regulate their own emotions.

If you are ready to empower your teen and help them stand in their own power by regulating their emotions, then keep following along! Throughout the rest of this chapter, we are going to share three ways you can teach your teen how to self-regulate. We're going to first help them get tougher skin, change their mindset, and then use specific tools to put it into action!

Build Resilience

Think about a time in your life where life was hard—maybe you wanted to give up, you were on your last leg, and everything seemed hopeless, but you kept going anyway. For me, it was being a single mom at 24 and losing the government assistance I was getting because I made $50 a month too much. I was in school full time, working part time, had just bought my first house, and now suddenly had to pay for groceries, and went from paying $20 per week for daycare to almost $200. I looked at my measly $1,600 per month paycheck and the more than $1,000 of expenses I now was responsible for. Talk about feeling hopeless and defeated...

Now, I could have gone to my boss and asked to back my hours down a bit to be back within the range to receive benefits. But I didn't want to rely on the government. I wanted to stand on my own feet and take care of myself and my son. So, I picked up two more jobs (maybe not the best option), and kept pushing forward. I was determined to make it and not have to go back to the government for help.

What drove me forward at this moment? Probably the same thing that drove you to get through your own tough experiences—resilience. Resilience is the ability to bounce back from setbacks and challenges. Sadly, this seems to be a skill that is seriously lacking in youth today. Don't just take my word for it. The stats don't lie. A December 2023 CNBC article said, "During the last two decades, youth suicide has increased significantly. From 2007 through 2021, suicide rates for Americans ages 10 to 24 rose 62%, according to the CDC."

Can we sit on that for a minute? 62%. What is the biggest change in teens' lives in the past 20 years? Social media. We are going to talk about the tech and online world in another chapter, so we won't dive into that now. However, I truly believe that the increase in youth suicide is because today's teens lack the maturity and resilience to handle rapid changes in technology and social media on their own.

So, how can you as a mom with teens develop resiliency in your kiddos? One of the biggest ways is by developing a growth mindset, which we're going to talk about in the next section. For now, let's focus on three things you can do.

Build a Supportive Environment

When we provide a supportive environment where our teen feels loved, supported, and safe, this allows them to take more risks, to try, and to put themselves out there because they don't have a fear around their relationship with their parents.

You can create this type of environment for your teen through open communication so your teens know they can share their struggles and successes with you. Encourage strong relationships with family, friends, and mentors who can provide emotional support. And create a safe space where teens feel comfortable discussing their feelings and challenges without judgment.

Provide Opportunities for Growth

What do I mean by this, you might ask? Well, when we provide an opportunity for our teens to take responsibility, or make decisions for themselves, we are giving them an opportunity to grow through problem solving, managing failure, setting realistic expectations, and giving them a sense of competence when they achieve something on their own. This is a great way for them to develop skills or resilience and perseverance!

This also means that we don't put a lot of pressure on our teens to achieve perfection. Instead, we praise them for their efforts and their failures. After all, failure truly is the best lesson. And failing at home, where we can protect, support, and love them, is much better than failing alone in the real world.

Encourage Healthy Habits and Self-Care

We all know that being healthy is important, but how does this help my teen be resilient? Well, when we are at our best, then so is our mind, and we are stronger than when we are tired, overstimulated, or consumed two bags of Reese's candy, a bag of Cheetos, and a two-liter bottle of pop. Our physical health plays a huge role in keeping our mental health healthy too!

So, promote regular physical activity, healthy eating, and sufficient sleep to support overall well-being. You can also teach stress management techniques such as mindfulness, deep breathing, and relaxation exercises, which we're going to talk about more in another section. Finally, one of the most important points for resilience is to emphasize the value of taking breaks, balancing responsibilities, and engaging in activities that bring joy and relaxation. Helping your teen know they don't have to do it all, that they can take breaks, and that they can say no to things will empower them for the rest of their lives.

Resiliency truly is a foundational piece of emotional intelligence. In the next section, we are going to discuss another essential piece that every teen MUST have to grow their emotional intelligence.

Encourage a Growth Mindset

I remember the first time my son came home and complained to me about all the things going wrong at school. Recess was terrible. Everyone got in trouble because of another kid, so nobody could play soccer. The teachers were out to get him. He suddenly hated math and reading and was just in a bad mood. I remember sitting there thinking, *What happened to my positive little kid who was always happy, loved everyone, was so "go-with-the-flow"...?*

I didn't understand who exchanged my happy, positive little boy for this Negative Nancy (sorry Nancy). And then it just went downhill from there. He started complaining more about almost everything. And then I'd talk to his friends' moms, and they'd say their boys were doing the same thing, and suddenly I saw this pattern that happened once they hit the double digits and were just about out of that "innocent kid" phase. They were ALL Negative Nancys!

In reality, that is true, but not because they suddenly changed. What happened was their cute little kid glasses that saw the world in rainbows and sunshine melted away. They became more aware of the world and the things going on around them. And they are HUMANs.

Did you know that it is human nature to be negative? To look for the bad instead of the good. In fact, if we have a bad experience, say at a restaurant, we are likely going to tell 10 people about it. If we have a good experience at that same restaurant, we will probably only tell about 1 or 2 people. This is how we are wired. Talk about a bummer for small businesses...

As parents, we don't want our kids to be these negative, whiny, complaining little monsters. We want them to be grateful and kind and positive and excited about life. And the only way that is going to happen is if we can teach our teens how to have a growth mindset.

This is one of the most powerful lessons anyone can ever learn, and it not only improves our teen's emotional intelligence but also gives them a superpower that will help them for the rest of their life. So, what is a growth mindset you might ask? It is the ability to view challenges as opportunities for growth rather than obstacles. It is like seeing the bright side of every situation.

Now, this doesn't come naturally to any of us, especially to teenagers, who are in this phase where it is cool to hate everything and everyone and all their friends are doing it too.

Here are some ways you can help develop a growth mindset in your teen.

Model It

Create a culture that exhibits this at home. If everyone in your home is negative with a fixed mindset, it is going to be really hard to change your teen's thinking. So, it starts with you!

Focus on Effort and Progress, Not Results

Focusing on the outcome will not foster a growth mindset. Instead, focus on the journey that leads to the outcome, including the achievements that happen and the progress made to get to the finish line. Think about the outcome as the reward for all the hard work and perseverance—if not for the effort, the result wouldn't happen.

This is also true when the outcome doesn't happen, because now instead of that failure bringing your teen to a negative place, they see the progress and effort and lessons they learned and can now go back and try again.

Practice Gratitude and Pay Attention to Words

The best way to develop a growth mindset is by immersing yourself in it. From the words you speak, to what you listen to, to who you hang out with. Substitute phrases like "not yet" or "I'm not there yet" for "can't" or "I'm not going to make it."

One of the most valuable things you can do with your teen is practice daily gratitude. This could be first thing in the morning, during lunch, at dinner, or even before bed. Having them write down and say out loud a few things they are grateful for every day can shift their mindset.

We've all heard the saying "You are the average of the five people you surround yourself with." I have heard this many times over the years, but when my pastor at church said it one day during a message, it hit me differently. It really made me evaluate who I was spending my time with and if they were the people I wanted to be like. The same goes for you and your teen. The people they spend the most time with are the ones who will influence them. So, it is important to help our teens see what healthy relationships look like, how to set boundaries, and to know their own goals and their value. We will talk more about this in a later chapter, but food for thought!

Our last section on self-regulation will give you concrete tools and strategies you can use with your teen to help them strengthen their mind and improve their emotional intelligence. Tools they can use anytime, anywhere, to empower them to be the best version of themselves!

Strategies to Manage Emotions

Now, I have to say, before I go too deep into this section, I know that you're probably thinking, "Ugh, Traci is going to talk to me about deep breathing exercises and woo-woo stuff that I see online all the time," and my answer to you is yes. Yes, I am. AND I'm also going to teach you how to do these things so that you get results and show you WHY it is important to teach your teen these strategies and tools to help them better manage their emotions.

Some of those simple activities, such as deep breathing, mindfulness, or physical activities like exercise, really are scientifically proven to help you better regulate your emotions. And remember, that is what emotional intelligence is all about. It is important for your teen to understand that it's okay to feel powerful emotions but that they can choose how to respond to them. And sometimes, when those emotions are very strong, we can't just talk ourselves down. We need actual physical techniques or exercises to do that will help us.

So, we are going to review three simple techniques that you can practice daily with your teen so they are more prepared to regulate their emotions when things get a little crazy, because they will.

Deep Breathing and Muscle Relaxation

One of my past coaches, who owns the Institute for Trauma and Psychological Safety, developed a technique she calls the *10 Second Protocol* for emotional regulation. It is an AMAZING program, and I highly recommend that if you need help to navigate your own trauma or your teen needs it, reach out to them. I make no claim to owning this process. The institute makes the method freely available on their website (no, I didn't steal it for this book, thank you!). Here's the process:

- Step #1: Inhale

- Step #2: Squeeze your body from your toes to the crown of your head (or selectively squeeze any part you desire). Then count to 5.

- Step #3: Exhale while relaxing all tensed body parts. Count to 5.

- Step #4: Take three slow breaths while moving your body in whichever way feels good. (Roll head, stretch neck, circle hips, etc.) Notice if any emotions/thoughts come up as you do this.

- Step #5: Repeat as many times as needed to feel your body stay relaxed (likely two to three times).

This exercise is a physical way for you to release thoughts, feelings, and emotions that are causing tension and stress. I suggest that you do this together with your teen. And yes, at first they might be like "Mom, this is stupid," but you can just laugh and say "It might be, but let's try it, anyway! What is the worst that could happen to us? We get a good chuckle and then move on with our day?"

Moving Your Body

I know when I get completely overwhelmed or overstimulated or plain stressed out, because I just want to run away. I want to get away from the situation, the environment, or the location I am in and get outside and move. Often, going on a walk, doing some yoga, or just doing something with the kids like throwing a ball or shooting hoops gets me regulated enough to have a clear mind and not feel like I'm coming out of my skin (anxiety is really fun…NOT).

I can tell you as a person who has experienced anxiety for years that physical movement and getting fresh air on a regular basis really keeps me in a much better head space the majority of the time. If your teen is high strung and has heightened emotions, getting out and moving may be the best thing for them to help them better regulate their emotions consistently.

Creative Outlets

If your teen is a creative person, then perhaps journaling, drawing, doing art, or engaging in other types of creative outlets may be a great option for them to better regulate their emotions. Especially if they have a hard time articulating their feelings, maybe they could *show* you instead through creativity. A dear friend of mine and someone I partner with in business owns an AMAZING company called *Teen Wise*, where she focuses on helping preteen to young adult girls navigate friendships, girl drama, and other challenges that young ladies face. And one thing she does with clients is a creative outlet. It is powerful, and the girls love it!

Journaling can be a powerful tool for regulating emotions. However, I would caution your teen to not just pour out all their negative thoughts. Have them keep that growth mindset in place, and perhaps after writing out the situation, their feelings about it, and so forth, then have them focus on what they can do, what emotions they would like to have in place of the negative ones, and maybe even do a grounding technique. A popular process is the 5-4-3-2-1 Method, where you identify five things you see, four things you feel, three things you hear, two things you smell, and one thing you taste. It helps you regulate by focusing on your senses instead of what you are feeling emotionally. This can help distract the brain from spiraling and going down the rabbit hole of darkness.

If you can at least set these foundations in place for your teen, they will be well on their way to having high emotional intelligence. The foundations are a must. Once you get them in place, you can then build on them. As for the other blocks of emotional intelligence, check out Chapter 10, YOUR Partner in Parenting, for resources to help!

Conclusion

Teens may resist talking about their emotions or feel uncomfortable at first. Be patient and consistent, and reassure them that their feelings are valid and important.

Teaching your teen emotional intelligence is a vital step in preparing them for adulthood. By recognizing and managing their emotions, developing empathy, and building resilience, your teen will be better equipped to navigate life's challenges and build meaningful relationships. Remember, your role as a parent is crucial in guiding them through this process, and your consistent support and example will make all the difference.

Put It Into Practice

Here are some activities that you can do with your teen to practice the things we discussed in this chapter and help you be on your way to having a great relationship with your teen!

1. JOINT ACTIVITY: Emotion Journaling

Set aside a time each day where you and your teen write in your own emotion journals, noting the emotions felt throughout the day, what triggered those emotions, and responses. At the end of the week, come together to discuss any patterns you both noticed in your emotions and reactions. This activity helps both mom and teen build self-awareness by reflecting on their emotional experiences.

2. SEPARATE ACTIVITY: "Who Am I?" Reflection

Have your teen create a "Who Am I?" reflection. Ask them to write about their strengths, weaknesses, likes, dislikes, values, and what makes them unique. They should also reflect on how these aspects influence their emotions and behavior in different situations. Meanwhile, moms can do a similar reflection about their own self-awareness journey.

3. TOGETHER EXERCISE: Practice Mindful Breathing

Practice mindful breathing together to help with emotional regulation. Find a quiet place, sit comfortably, and practice deep breathing exercises. Start with simple techniques like inhaling for a count of 4, holding for 4, and exhaling for 4. Discuss how you both feel before and after the exercise, and talk about how this technique can help when feeling overwhelmed or stressed.

4. ROLE-PLAY: Handling Emotional Triggers

Create a role-play scenario where the teen has to manage an emotionally triggering situation. For example, one scenario could be a disagreement with a friend. The mom plays the role of the friend who is being difficult, and the teen must practice recognizing their emotions, using a calming technique, and responding in a composed manner. After the role-play, discuss how they felt and what strategies they used to stay calm.

Don't forget your workbook! It's so good!

5

FRIENDSHIP FOUNDATIONS

GUIDING YOUR TEEN IN RELATIONSHIPS

Have you ever been head over heels for someone, but deep down, you knew it wasn't a great relationship? Or maybe you were blinded by love? Or had this desire to "fix" that person? No? Just me, huh? I look back at my dating life when I was in high school, and let me tell you, it wasn't pretty. It was always the "bad" boy, the one who came from a bad situation or didn't have the best family. I wanted to "fix" them, to be the Princess Charming who came in and saved the day. Unfortunately, it never actually worked. Instead, I would be the one they would leave completely heartbroken, questioning what I had done wrong.

It wasn't until years later that I learned it was never *me*. It was the relationship that wasn't healthy. I didn't respect myself enough to put up the boundaries that were needed to protect myself. Instead, I let significant others walk all over me, taking advantage of my kindness, generosity, and emotions. I wish I had learned what a healthy relationship was supposed to be like, and that I was important enough to be in one.

Now, I get to help you empower your teen with the knowledge and armor that will help them understand and know what a healthy relationship is, whether it is a significant other, a friend, a co-worker, a supervisor, or even a family member.

Understanding Healthy Relationships

Before we can dive into the *how*, we need to talk about the *what*. What are healthy relationships? Healthy relationships require mutual respect, trust, boundaries, and open communication. For teens, learning how to navigate friendships and romantic relationships is crucial for their emotional and social development. By fostering these skills, you can help your teen develop the ability to form and maintain positive relationships throughout their life.

I truly believe that if we were all taught how to create and maintain healthy relationships from a young age, there would be less divorce, fewer mental health issues, and more happy people in this world. When you are in a toxic relationship, it is draining. It brings you down, tears you up, and spits you out. We've all seen it—when someone goes through a friendship or relationship breakup, they get worn out, depressed, and miserable. I know that none of you want this for your kids, so let's get into how you can teach your teen to have a healthy relationship.

We believe that there are four foundational pillars to a healthy relationship: Boundaries, Mutual Respect, Trust, and Support and Encouragement. Now, you might ask, "But what about open communication?" Yes! Open communication is an essential pillar, but these other four pillars are the prerequisites for open communication. To have open communication, you have to have good boundaries, respect each other, trust each other, and provide support and encouragement for one another.

For this chapter, we are going to focus on our third pillar of healthy relationships, which is Boundaries. So, let's dive into the what, how, and why of teaching your teen to create healthy boundaries in their relationships!

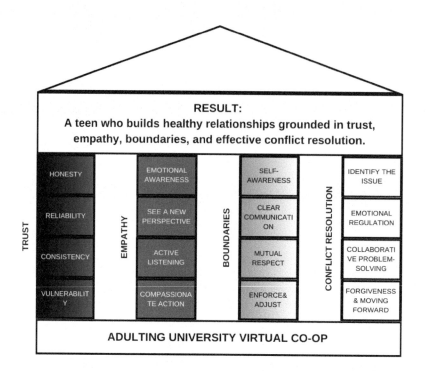

Pillar #1: Boundaries

When we talk about boundaries in a relationship, we are talking about putting up barriers to maintain self-respect, to protect us from emotional harm, and to avoid toxic, hurtful relationships. It is crucial that our teens understand how to create their own boundaries and respect others' boundaries. Unhealthy relationships can go both ways. It isn't always the other person with the boundary problem. Helping our kids respect boundaries is a crucial part of this process.

There are three different types of boundaries: emotional, physical, and digital.

Emotional Boundaries

Emotional boundaries are boundaries we put in place to protect our emotions, express our emotions, and say no to others' emotional baggage.

Teaching our teens to protect their emotional space is a huge step in their emotional intelligence journey (discussed in our preceding chapter). It is telling our teens that they are allowed to recognize their own emotional needs, and to take time for themselves to process through those emotions without feeling guilty.

We can teach our teens about this type of boundary through clear communication and using statements like "I need some alone time right now to process my feelings" or "I don't want to talk about that right now."

This boundary also allows teens to express their feelings and emotions in a healthy manner instead of keeping things bottled up inside. Too often, we tiptoe, or "walk on eggshells" as the saying goes, to not hurt others' feelings, and instead we take the brunt of the hurt and toxicity by doing this. When we teach our teens that it is okay to express their feelings in a healthy way, we encourage them to communicate their needs and feelings honestly, which creates respect and understanding in relationships.

And finally, this boundary will allow our teens to not feel like they have to take on everyone else's emotional burdens at the expense of their own well-being. This doesn't mean they can't choose to step into their friend's issues. It simply means they will know how to do it in a way that is healthy for them.

Physical Boundaries

Physical boundaries are those boundaries that help to protect your personal space and your physical well-being.

These boundaries are ones I feel most people are the least comfortable in setting, especially teens, and especially when adults are involved. Sometimes it is easier to say "I'm upset or angry right now" than telling grandma you don't like to be hugged. However, both are very important. In fact, with physical boundaries, there are boundaries for our personal space, like our bedroom and privacy. Then there is the big one of consent for physical touch, which covers everything from a simple hug to bigger decisions around sex. And finally, there is the aspect of boundaries to just protect your overall physical well-being, meaning not falling into uncomfortable activities that could put you in harm's way.

All three physical boundaries are so important for our kids to understand and know not only to protect themselves but to protect others as well. We can teach our kids about this type of boundary by helping them know what they do and don't want regarding physical space, touch, and safety.

Once they start to really understand what they are okay with and what they're not okay with, we can then teach the language around setting those boundaries. For example:

- "Please knock before entering my room," or "I need some space right now, please," or "Can we stand/sit a little farther apart? I'm not comfortable with people standing too close to me."

- "I don't feel comfortable hugging people I just met," or "I would rather not be touched. Can we keep things nonphysical?"

- "I don't think this is something I should do right now, it is going to put my safety at risk," or "I'm not comfortable participating in things that put my safety at risk, so I'm going to have to pass this time."

When it comes to sexual contact, here are a few things teens could say depending on the situation:

- If they're not ready for that type of physical contact:

  ○ "I'm not ready for this, and I want to wait," or "I care about you, but I'm not ready to take this step," or "I'm not comfortable with this right now, and I need you to respect that."

- If they just want to wait for that type of physical contact:

  ○ "I want to wait until I'm older/more certain before doing this," or "I think it's important for us to wait until we're both ready," or "I'm choosing to wait because it's important to me."

- If they want to emphasize the boundary because maybe the first approach isn't being respected, they could say things like this:

  ○ "I'm not ready for sex, and I need you to respect my decision," or "I've decided to wait, and I'm asking you to support me in that," or "No, I'm not comfortable with this, and I'm not going to do it."

It is important for teens to understand that relationships sometimes fall apart when someone sets a boundary, but that's okay. It isn't their fault. When we raise our sons and daughters to be confident, be secure, and set healthy boundaries, then they can be proud of sticking to them even when other people don't respect them or choose to leave. They will know they stood up for what they believe in, what keeps them safe, and what keeps them from doing what they don't want to do. We need to celebrate and praise our teens when they stick to a boundary!

Digital Boundaries

Digital boundaries are ones that help keep your teen safe online. This could be from scammers, fake accounts, false information, and even online bullying. It can also be a boundary to help protect their mental health and well-being.

Digital boundaries are so important these days! We're going to talk more about staying safe online in a later chapter, but here I want to highlight the different boundaries that your teen can put into place to protect themselves online.

Having our teens understand the importance of limiting screen time, protecting their privacy online, and even respecting digital communication is crucial. This is one of those areas that gets most teens in a lot of trouble.

I don't know about your kids, but my son LOVES playing video games. If we didn't help him put healthy boundaries in place, he would play all day, every day. And when he has too much screen time in a day, he becomes a completely different kid. He becomes lazy, unmotivated, and sassy, and his entire demeanor changes. For us, when he acts this way, we know it is time for a screen/digital detox.

The easiest solution is to have digital boundaries by only allowing so much screen time in a day, saying that phones go off at a certain time at night, and during dinner and family time we put down our phones...

The next step is making sure our teens understand the risks and dangers that live in the online world. Helping them put healthy boundaries in place to protect their privacy and information in the online space will help them the rest of their lives!

There are three ways you can teach your teen boundaries, and we're going to explore those now!

How to Teach Boundaries

We focus on three primary strategies to teach boundaries: modeling behavior, open communication, and providing guidance and support. Let's take a deeper look at each of these!

Modeling Behavior

If you want your teen to have boundaries, then the number one way for them to learn is from you. This is a very common theme you will see throughout the book, by the way! It truly is the best way to learn almost everything we talk about in this book, because the way mom sets or doesn't set boundaries is going to show her kids how to set or not have boundaries.

And as women, this can sometimes be something we have never done before. I never had boundaries as a young person. I let everyone walk all over me and take advantage of me. I was a "Yes, ma'am" kind of girl who never said no (even when I wanted to), and it was EXHAUSTING!!

You know what? My mom did the SAME THING! And I love my mom. We are very close, but a lot of my toxic and unhealthy traits came from her not having healthy boundaries in place. And I know she wanted desperately for me to not make the same mistakes, to be confident, and to stand up for myself, but she didn't model that behavior because her mom didn't model that behavior for her (see where I'm going with this??).

Now, I want you to hear me. I am not placing blame on anyone, not you, not me, not my mom, not her mom... We aren't doing this on purpose. We just were never taught the importance of boundaries or even how to put them in place! AND that gets to change now!

We get to put healthy boundaries in place for ourselves around our mental, physical, and digital well-being and show our kids what that looks like. We get to have conversations with them about why we are setting those boundaries and what that's going to do for us, and we get to SHOW them, not just tell them, why boundaries are important.

Open Communication

Open communication is the next part of the puzzle of healthy boundaries. We have to have conversations with our children. We have to ask open-ended questions and dive into what boundaries are and why they are important, and ask them about where they would want boundaries in their life.

Ask them questions like this:

- "How do you feel when someone pressures you to do something you're not comfortable with? What boundary could you set in that situation?"

- "What activities or situations make you feel overwhelmed or stressed? How can we set limits to protect your mental health?"

- "When you're feeling upset or anxious, what kind of space or support do you need? How can we make sure you get that?"

- "What are your thoughts on physical touch, like hugs or holding hands? How do you let someone know if you're not comfortable with it?"

- "If someone invades your personal space, what would be a good way to handle that situation?"

- "How do you feel about saying 'no' to activities or situations that make you uncomfortable physically, like sports or being in crowds?"

- "How do you decide what to share online and what to keep private? What boundaries do you want to set for your digital life?"

- "What do you think about the time you spend on social media? How can we create a balance that feels healthy for you?"

- "If someone messages you in a way that makes you uncomfortable, how would you respond? What boundaries do you want to have in place for online interactions?"

- "Are there any areas in your life where you feel you need stronger boundaries? How can we work together to help you feel more confident in setting them?"

- "How do you feel about standing up for yourself when you need to? What are some ways you can practice setting boundaries?"

We have to prioritize having these conversations with our kids—and actually talk to them to understand what they feel is acceptable and what they feel is not with boundaries.

Remember in Chapter 3 where we laid that foundation in communication to have healthy communication with your teen? Now we get to put that into action by having these conversations with our teens!

Once we have conversations around boundaries, then comes our next and final step, which brings everything together!

Providing Guidance and Support

Providing guidance and support is the third and final step to teaching our teens about boundaries. Now that we are modeling boundaries in our own life, and having conversations with them about the boundaries they would like to set in their life, we get to provide guidance on how to set boundaries and support them through their journey.

Think of this as the education piece of the puzzle. This is where we educate them on the different boundaries and help them identify where they feel they need to put a boundary in place.

We then help educate and guide them on the language to use to share those boundaries, and stand behind them.

Then, it is our job to support and encourage our teens to stick to those boundaries, even if the boundaries apply to us, which they might—so be prepared! They may want more space from you or more privacy, and even if we don't like it, we need to respect it if it is a reasonable request.

When we witness our teens sticking to their guns in a relationship, praise and celebrate that with them. Will they feel embarrassed when you're jumping up and down and celebrating them? Probably! Will they secretly love it and feel good about it? Absolutely! However, they may set another boundary that you can no longer do in public, ha ha!

Teaching these boundaries is so important, but what happens when people challenge our boundaries? How can our teens handle when the boundary they set isn't being respected or is getting pushback?

Handling Boundary Violations

Unfortunately, just because we set boundaries doesn't automatically mean everyone is going to respect them. Sometimes it's simply because they didn't know about the boundary, whereas other times they know but don't care.

Here are five steps to help your teen navigate these difficult situations.

Step #1: Recognize Boundary Violations. Help your teen recognize when their boundaries are being crossed, like feeling uncomfortable, disrespected, or pressured. Discuss specific situations where people might violate their boundaries, such as someone repeatedly ignoring their request for personal space or pressuring them to do something they're uncomfortable with.

Role-play scenarios where someone crosses a boundary, and have your teen identify the violation. For example, simulate a situation where a friend continuously interrupts them, then discuss how this affects their personal space and feelings.

Step #2: Assertively Communicate the Violation. Encourage your teen to express their feelings and needs clearly without blaming or accusing the other person. For example, "I feel disrespected when you ignore my request for privacy. Please knock before entering my room." Teach them to remain calm and firm in their communication, even if the other person reacts negatively.

Practice assertive communication through role-playing. Have your teen rehearse different ways to address boundary violations using "I" statements and maintaining a calm tone.

Step #3: Set Consequences for Continued Violations. If someone repeatedly violates a boundary, discuss the importance of setting consequences to protect themselves. This might involve limiting contact with the person or leaving a situation, or involving a trusted adult.

An example could be if a friend continues to pressure them after being asked to stop, they might say, "If you keep pushing me to do this, I'll need to take a break from our friendship." To be clear, it isn't a threat but a consequence if they keep crossing our boundary.

Work together to create a list of potential consequences for different boundary violations. Discuss when and how to implement these consequences if needed.

Step #4: Seek Support When Needed. Teach your teen that it's okay to seek help from trusted adults, such as parents, teachers, and counselors, if they're struggling to enforce their boundaries or if the violation is severe. Encourage them to talk to friends who respect their boundaries and can provide emotional support.

Identify a support network with your teen. Make a list of people they can turn to if they need help handling a boundary violation. Discuss how and when to reach out for support.

Step #5: Reflect and Learn. After addressing a boundary violation, encourage your teen to reflect on the situation. Ask them what worked, what didn't, and how they felt about their response. Help them consider if they need to adjust their boundaries or communication strategies based on the experience.

Have your teen keep a journal to document situations where their boundaries were challenged, how they responded, and what they learned from the experience. Use these reflections as a basis for discussions on improving their boundary setting skills.

It is important to make sure our kids are prepared for situations where people test their boundaries, so practicing at home together can be a great way to give them practice so they feel more prepared when those situations arise!

The last piece of the boundary puzzle is to make sure our teens also know to respect others' boundaries. Emphasize the importance of respecting others' boundaries in return. Discuss how mutual respect is one of the foundations of healthy relationships. Encourage them to consider how they would feel if someone crossed their boundaries, and how they can be more mindful of others' limits. You could even role-play scenarios where your teen is on the receiving end of a boundary being set by someone else. Discuss how to respond respectfully and with understanding.

Conclusion

Setting boundaries isn't just about saying "no." It's about helping your teen build a strong sense of self and respect for others. As teens learn to navigate the tricky waters of friendships and relationships, these skills will be their life raft, keeping them afloat when things become stormy. By guiding them through the process of setting and maintaining healthy boundaries, you're not just teaching them to stand up for themselves—you're giving them the tools to create meaningful, lasting connections with the people in their lives.

Remember, you're not just their parent—you're their coach, cheerleader, and occasional reality check. Your support is key as your teen learns to balance their own needs with the expectations of others. And guess what? You're doing an amazing job.

Now that we've tackled the emotional side of things, it's time to switch gears. In the next chapter, we'll dive into the world of critical thinking—because helping your teen sharpen their mind is just as important as helping them guard their heart. Get ready to equip them with the skills to analyze, evaluate, and make decisions like a pro. Let's build those brain muscles!

Put It Into Practice

Here are some activities that you can do with your teen to practice the things we discussed in this chapter and help your teen be well on their way to having healthy relationships and friendships!

1. JOINT ACTIVITY: Create a "Boundary Map"

Together, create a "Boundary Map" for different areas of life, such as friendships, romantic relationships, family interactions, and online behavior. Use a large sheet of paper or a whiteboard and draw circles representing different levels of comfort and closeness. For example, the innermost circle might represent family, the next circle close friends, and so on. Discuss what types of behaviors, communication, and physical space feel appropriate in each circle.

2. SEPARATE ACTIVITY: Encourage Journaling

Encourage your teen to keep a journal where they reflect on their relationships and interactions each day. They can write about moments when they felt their boundaries were respected or crossed, how they handled those situations, and what they might do differently next time. Meanwhile, moms can do a similar reflection on how they set and maintain boundaries in their own relationships.

3. TOGETHER EXERCISE: Observe Boundaries

Watch a movie or TV show together, and as you watch, point out characters who either respect or violate boundaries. Discuss how those characters' actions affected their relationships and what they could have done differently. Afterward, create a list of "Boundary Role Models" from the show—characters who demonstrate healthy boundaries—and talk about what your teen can learn from them.

4. ROLE-PLAY: Practice Saying "No"

Create a role-play scenario where your teen has to say "no" assertively in a variety of situations. For example, a friend is pressuring them to do something they're not comfortable with or a peer is trying to invade their personal space. The mom plays the role of the friend or peer, and the teen practices responding with a clear, firm "no" while maintaining respect. After each role-play, discuss how it felt to set that boundary and what other strategies your teen could use.

Still missing this amazing resource!? Grab it now!

6

THINK LIKE A PRO

SHARPENING YOUR TEEN'S MIND

Did you know that a staggering 60% of employers report that recent graduates from both high school and even college lack critical thinking and problem solving skills? These skills are an essential part of adulthood, and sadly, many teens are growing up seriously lacking these skills.

There's a lot of debate as to why this is, many blaming social media, technology, the removal of good old textbooks as the primary learning tool, video games, and so on. Regardless of the root cause, although I'd say it is likely a combination of all the above, the reality is that we as parents have to help our kids learn how to be critical thinkers.

Unless you want little Johnny living in your basement playing video games the rest of your life, you likely want him to spread his wings and leave the nest at some point. This means he is going to need to get a job, and with the current stats as they are from the employers who could hire little Johnny someday, we have a lot of work to do! And it will not get better. The job market is going to continue to be competitive, meaning the ability to think critically and solve problems creatively is more important than ever.

This chapter is dedicated to helping you, as a homeschool mom, equip your teen with these vital skills. By teaching your teen how to analyze situations, make informed decisions, and be creative, you can prepare them for success in the real world. But before we get into the nitty gritty, let's break down what critical thinking really is.

Understanding Critical Thinking

What comes to mind when you think of critical thinking? It is one of those things that isn't always as simple as it sounds. On the surface, critical thinking involves the ability to analyze information objectively, evaluate that information, and make reasoned judgments or decisions. I know, it is a very professional-sounding definition. However, when we go beyond that, critical thinking is really the ability to navigate life. Think about it. If you don't know how to think critically, you will go through life believing everything you see and hear. You will just buy into whatever sounds good. You will become a follower, not a leader.

I like to think of *The Lego Movie*. Emit is the perfect example of what it looks like to not have critical thinking skills. He starts off the movie being like everyone else, following the directions President Business gave him, questioning nothing. He goes through life unaware of all the nefarious things going on around him, believing he has friends. Emit thinks he is happy, only to find out that most people don't even remember him because he fits the mold so well that he isn't even memorable.

Like in many movies, Emit has this self-realization that his life has been a lie, and when the curtain finally peels back, he sees the truth of everything. Throughout his journey of being "the chosen," he surrounds himself with master builders who help him open his mind to possibilities, to question things, and to begin to "think outside the box."

SPOILER ALERT

By the end of the movie, Emit has an epiphany when he sees the truth behind Legoland, and he is now seeing and doing things like a master builder, aka a critical thinker! Of course, he then uses these new abilities to save Legoland, not by destroying Lord Business but by using reasoning and logic to help him see what he has been doing is wrong. Then everyone lives happily ever after, until the alien invasion of course.

To me, this is the perfect description of critical thinking. It is the ability to see through lies, deceptions, and bias. To know how to find the truth, then how to interpret the truth and the information to make informed decisions. Without this skill, we would all be like pre–master builder Emit. We could not think for ourselves. Like robots, we would just follow everything, never questioning things, never learning.

Do you want your kid to be a robot? My guess is probably not...

So what does it take to become a master builder (critical thinker)? Well, like you've probably guessed, we have pillars and blocks for that too!

The essential pillars of critical thinking are Research, Evaluate Evidence, Critical Analysis, and Effective Decision Making. If your teen has these, not only will they be a master of critical thinking, but they also will be a thoughtful, informed individual capable of making well-reasoned decisions and solving complex problems. Who doesn't want that?

Just like in other chapters, we will not cover all the pillars here. If you have to focus on just one area, the place to start is the Research pillar. The four blocks that make up that pillar are Credible Sources, Effective Searches, Differentiating Sources, and Citations and Plagiarism. For this chapter, we will focus on credible sources.

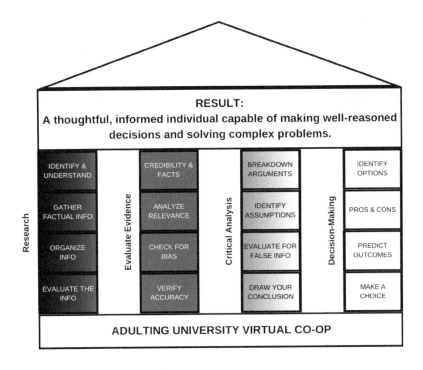

Block #1: Credible Sources

I remember the first time my son really argued with me about something. He was adamant that the information he was sharing was the die-hard truth. There was no backing down, because one of his friends had said it, so it MUST be true. He was probably about 9, almost 10, when this happened. Finally, I had to ask, "Well, have you looked it up yourself?" He stopped and looked at me a little funny, and replied, "No . . . because so and so told me it, so I don't have to."

So I said, "Well let's see what we can find online about it, just to make sure." He agreed, and when we looked it up—believe it or not—his friend was wrong. Needless to say, my son felt very sheepish about the whole situation, while also frustrated because he didn't understand why his friend would lie.

We had an entire conversation about his friend and agreed they were probably not intentionally lying. Instead, they probably heard it from someone else they trusted, who heard it from another person, and so on. The core lesson in all of this was to make sure the information you are getting and the things you choose to believe come from a credible source.

I don't have to tell you why this is important, but I'm going to anyway. Why? Because I can (hehe)—no, seriously, it's because it is something that we don't talk about enough in our country. And if you haven't noticed, I wrote this book in 2024, right smack in the middle of a presidential election season. Enough said, right?

Here's the thing. Our youth today have become so accustomed to just accepting information from authority figures, from influencers, from friends, from professors, from people they watch online. And it has caused an entire generation and beyond to not be able to think critically, or to think for themselves.

When we go through life just accepting things, or believing information we see or hear without verifying that the source is a legitimate one for that information, then we are really doing ourselves a disservice and, honestly, everyone around us too.

I don't want to bring politics into this book, but I believe it is important to mention when we are talking about this subject in particular, because with elections and voting on issues or leaders, the credibility of sources has a huge impact on our country, our state, our city, and our lives. And when you have young people not doing their research, not verifying the information that they are hearing or seeing, then they are uneducated on decisions that could impact their life.

Let's go back to Emit. He read all the books, read all the training manuals, and watched all the shows, and he believed everything to be true because it came from leadership. Once he peeled back the curtain, he saw that the "leadership" wasn't a very credible source of information, because they had an agenda of keeping everyone in order. (Pretty deep stuff I know!)

This is why I like to focus on this block first, because before you can even think critically about anything, or make informed decisions, you have to know where the information is coming from and whether it is a credible source.

So, let's talk about three things you can do with your teen to help them break through misinformation and get to the truth from credible sources!

Understand What Makes a Source Credible

If you want to know what information comes from a credible source, then you need to identify what makes a credible source. It starts with looking into five areas: author credentials, publication reputation, website domain, source citations, and objective tone.

Author Credentials

The first step is to look at the author and their credentials to see if they are credible or not. Have your teen ask and answer questions like these: Is the author an expert in the field? Do they have the necessary academic background or professional experience?

For example, imagine you're watching a YouTube video about how to fix your bike. Would you trust the advice from someone who says "Well, I've never actually fixed a bike before, but I think this might work" or from someone who runs a bike repair shop and has been fixing bikes for 10 years? Just like with bike repair, when you're reading something online, it's important to know if the person giving the advice actually knows what they're talking about. Look for authors who have experience or education in the field they're writing about.

Publication Reputation

This one can be a little challenging these days, because many of the "reputable publications" that existed before are not quite as reliable as they used to be and often communicate opinions, bias, and misinformation. However, it can still be an important step to determining credibility. Here is a question you can teach your teen to ask: Is it a peer-reviewed journal, a well-known newspaper, or an established website? Credible publications "typically" have a reputation for accuracy and reliability.

Here's an example... Think about your favorite restaurant. You trust their food because they've built an excellent reputation over time. Now imagine a new food truck shows up in town. It might be awesome, but you're not sure yet because it doesn't have a reputation. In the same way, when you read something online, it's like eating at a restaurant with a reputation for quality. Publications like *The New York Times* or *National Geographic* are like that favorite restaurant—they've earned trust because they consistently serve up accurate, well-researched information. A random blog with no reputation is like that new food truck—you don't really know if you can trust it yet.

Website Domain

Just like publication reputation, this one can be a little tricky, especially if you grew up like I did where the Internet was relatively new and it wasn't easy to get a domain or a website like it is today. And when I was in school, we were taught that certain websites were always reliable because of their domain extension, Like .edu, .gov, and .org. However, today those aren't even 100% reliable.

In fact, I could have bought an AdultingUniversity.edu domain for my website if I wanted to, but the parameters that used to exist around reliability aren't really black and white anymore. So it is important to teach your teens to be cautious of websites with certain domain extensions. While .edu (educational institutions) and .gov (government websites) are generally reliable, your teens should evaluate .com and .org sites on a case-by-case basis.

For example, imagine you're shopping online for a new pair of sneakers. You find an amazing deal on a website you've never heard of before, like Sneakers-R-Us.xyz. It sounds a little sketchy, right? But if you find those same sneakers on a trusted site like Nike.com or Amazon.com, you feel more confident making the purchase. The same thing applies to website domains. Sites ending in .edu or .gov are like shopping at well-known stores—they're usually reliable because they're educational institutions or government websites. But websites with endings like .com or .org can be like that unknown sneaker site—you need to check them out carefully to make sure they're legit.

Source Citations

This one is big. If you are looking at information and sources are spouting "facts," data, and other information, make sure they are citing where they got that information. Credible sources often reference other trustworthy sources, studies, or data, which adds to their reliability. So, make sure you are verifying where information was obtained.

For example, let's say you're writing a history report, and you say "The moon landing was fake, according to my friend Joe." Now, Joe might be a cool guy, but is he really a reliable source for historical facts? Instead, if you cite a history book that references NASA's records, people are more likely to trust your report. In the same way, when you're reading something, check if the author backs up claims with citations from other credible sources. It's like making sure your friend Joe got his info from someone who actually knows about space travel—like an astronaut or a scientist.

Objective Tone

Finally, your last step in determining what makes a source credible is the tone. I believe this is one that trips up our youth more than anything else, especially in today's world where bias and opinions thread throughout a huge portion of information. Teach your teen to look for information that is presented objectively, meaning without an agenda or bias. The source should provide balanced views and consider a variety of perspectives.

Let's say you're watching two YouTube reviews of the latest video game. One reviewer says, "This game is the worst thing ever! Only idiots would play it." The other reviewer says, "While the graphics are great, the gameplay can feel repetitive. Some players might enjoy it, but others might not." Which review do you trust more? The second one, right? That's because it's balanced. In the same way, credible sources are like that second reviewer—they present the facts and different perspectives, letting you make up your own mind instead of trying to force an opinion on you.

Once your teen can identify and understand what makes a source credible, the next step is to learn how to evaluate sources, which is what we're going to talk about next!

Evaluating Sources

The next step in helping your teen identify credible sources is by evaluating sources. This is a little different from our previous step because now we have done some surface-level research and evaluation to see if a source is credible, but here we get into the information side!

There are two main things you need to teach your teen about evaluating sources of information online. They need to check for bias, and they need to cross-reference the information. Let's look at each of these individually.

Check for Bias

When was the last time you read or watched something that was supposed to be "factual" but was instead filled with the writer's opinions, views, or bias? If I had to guess, I'd say it was sometime in the past few hours, if not minutes.

In the age of information that we currently live in, we are drowning in bias. Bias is a tendency to favor one side, perspective, or group over another in a way that comes off unfair or misleading. This bias can often lead to what we call *fake news*, or false information. Now, this can become a VERY slippery slope for our youth, especially since they were born into this world with an iPhone in their hand.

Of course, bias comes to mind when we think of things like the news, social media, advertisements, and political campaigns. However, what really seems to suck in our teens are websites, blogs, forums, discussion boards, and influencers.

The top places that teens hang out are platforms like TikTok, YouTube, and Instagram. These platforms are filled with influencers, celebrities, and people who teens look up to or idolize but don't always put out unbiased information. And many times, that information is incorrect.

Have you ever watched some of those videos online where some random guy is going around asking teens or young adults simple questions, or asking about things going on in the world? And when that young person, bless their heart, opens their mouth, a whole lot of dumb comes out? And your mouth drops to the floor because you can't believe that they didn't know the answer, or spouted some completely ignorant information that is 100% not true? You want to know why that happens? Let me tell you.

It is because the youth today don't know how to identify bias and false information. They don't know how to know if something is fact or fiction because someone they respect and look up to, like Taylor Swift, says something about politics or religion or the environment or whatever the topic is, and now they assume it is absolutely true. Then you get this entire generation of cancel culture and things spiral, then you end up in the society and world that is America today.

So how do you change that?

First, we have to help our teens understand that not everything they see online is true, and that not every belief or word that comes out of someone's mouth is completely factual, including our own. We have our own biases, and we can often push those onto our children instead of letting them have their own opinions and views. Let's look at three ways to teach your teen how to recognize bias.

#1: Define and Identify. Before your teen can recognize bias, they first need to know that it exists, what it is, and the different types of bias. Help them understand that bias can be intentional or unintentional, and that it can influence how people present and perceive information.

There are three main types of bias they need to recognize when in an online space:

- *Confirmation Bias*: This is when people seek or interpret information in a way that confirms their existing beliefs. Explain that teens might unconsciously focus on information that supports their views and ignore what contradicts them. Example: If a teen believes that a certain celebrity is always right, they might only read articles that praise that celebrity and ignore any negative reports.

- *Media Bias*: Discuss how news outlets or websites might lean toward a particular political or social perspective, which can color the information they present. Example: Show how different news outlets report on the same event in different ways, emphasizing or omitting certain details to fit their narrative.

- *Cultural Bias*: Explain that cultural background can influence how people perceive information and events, leading to a biased viewpoint. Example: Discuss how holidays or traditions are portrayed differently in various cultures and how that can lead to a biased understanding.

Once teens understand bias, they can then look for it using our next step.

#2: Practice Makes Perfect. Once teens know what they are looking for, then comes the fun part of putting it to practice using a technique called *critical reading*. This is a process where you are looking for red flags as you read that can help you determine if this information is credible or not.

Here are three things you can do to teach your teen how to read critically:

- *Question the Source*: Encourage teens to ask "Who wrote this? What might be their purpose or agenda?" Teach them to look at the background of the author and the publication to assess whether there might be any biases influencing the content.

- *Look for Loaded Language*: Explain that biased sources often use emotionally charged language to influence the reader. Words like "outrageous," "unbelievable," or "disgraceful" can signal a biased perspective. Example: Compare two headlines about the same event—one that uses neutral language and one that uses loaded language—and discuss how they make the reader feel differently about the event.

- *Check for Balance*: Teach teens to notice if only one side of an issue is being presented. Ask them to consider if there might be another perspective that's not being discussed. Example: Read an article together, and ask the teen to identify what perspective is being presented and if there might be other viewpoints that are missing.

Now your teen is ready for the final step in checking for bias, which is to know their own bias.

#3: Know Your Own Bias. Knowing how to spot other people's bias is great, but there is one more person's bias you have to be aware of, and that is your own personal bias. We all have our own biases, and when we are teaching our kids these skills, it is important that they also understand and know their own biases.

There are two things you can do to help your teen identify their own bias. One is to encourage your teen to think about their own biases. Ask them to consider how their background, experiences, and beliefs might influence how they perceive information. This helps them become more aware of how bias can shape their own thinking. Another is to just have an open conversation about how everyone has biases, but that recognizing them is the first step to minimizing their impact on how we understand the world.

Now that we have been able to help our teens learn all about bias as part of their process for evaluating information, we're ready to tackle cross-referencing!

Cross-Reference

The last step of the evaluation is to cross-reference the information we have found. Teach teens the importance of checking multiple sources before forming an opinion.

Cross-referencing helps them see different perspectives and reduces the impact of any single biased source.

Let's say you hear a rumor at school that there's no homework in any class tomorrow. It sounds too good to be true, so you check with a few other classmates. One friend says, "Yeah, I heard the same thing from another student." But then you ask your teacher directly, and they confirm that homework is still due. You've just cross-referenced the information and found out that the rumor wasn't true.

When researching online, it's the same idea—don't just trust the first thing you read. Look for other credible sources that confirm the information. If you find multiple trustworthy websites saying the same thing, it's more likely to be accurate.

Now that we have evaluated the information, we are ready to make an informed decision, and that leads us to our third and final step for teaching our teens about credible sources.

Apply and Reflect

We have gone through the process of understanding what makes a source credible and discussed evaluating that source and information for credibility. We are now ready to make an informed decision or opinion with the information we have.

This is our third step, where we are ready to apply our knowledge and reflect on our decisions and choices. It's a great time to have your teen put into practice what they have learned. Assign some research projects for them to do to test their credibility skills!

Have them explain their process and why they chose the sources they did and how they determined the credibility. Then, provide them with feedback on their choices and discuss any discrepancies or challenges they faced.

The final tip I would give to teach your teen about credible sources and information is to encourage ongoing skepticism. Encourage them to maintain a healthy skepticism about the information they encounter, especially online. Teach them to question the source of information and its potential motives. Remind them that credibility can change. A once-reliable source may become less so, and new credible sources may emerge.

Conclusion

The ability to find and assess credible sources is so important for your teen's critical thinking. Teaching your teen critical thinking and problem solving skills is essential for their success in the real world. You can help your teen become a confident and capable decision maker by encouraging their understanding of credibility, helping them learn to evaluate sources and information, and asking them to put their skills into practice. By implementing these strategies and activities, your teen will go from the simple, nonindependent thinker Emit to a master builder, with all their own thoughts and opinions. They will see the truth behind the curtain!

As we move forward, we're not just sharpening our teens' minds—we're ensuring they're mentally equipped for the journey ahead. In the next chapter, we'll dive into the vital world of mental health, exploring how you can empower your teen to prioritize their well-being and build a strong foundation for a healthy, resilient mind.

Put It Into Practice

Here are some activities that you can do with your teen to practice the things we discussed in this chapter and help you be on your way to having a great relationship with your teen!

1. JOINT ACTIVITY: "Fact vs. Fiction" Challenge

Together, choose a current event or topic of interest and find three different articles or sources that discuss it. Sit down with your teen and go through each source, analyzing the author's credentials, the publication's reputation, and any potential biases. Use a checklist to evaluate the credibility of each source. Discuss which source seems most reliable and why.

2. SEPARATE ACTIVITY: Media Comparison

Ask your teen to compare how different media outlets report on the same event. They should select two or three different news sources (e.g., a newspaper, a TV news channel, and an online blog) and then analyze how each one presents the story. Have them note any differences in language, tone, and the facts presented. They should then write a brief reflection on which source they believe to be the most credible and why.

3. TOGETHER EXERCISE: Analyzing Social Media

Spend some time together going through social media posts, particularly those that share news or opinions on current events. Discuss the credibility of the posts by evaluating the sources they reference and identifying any signs of bias. Use this as an opportunity to talk about how to navigate social media critically and avoid misinformation.

4. ROLE-PLAY: Debating the Facts

Create a role-play scenario where one person (the teen) must argue for a position using only credible sources, whereas the other person (the mom) plays the role of someone using biased or noncredible sources. The teen must identify and point out the flaws in the noncredible arguments and provide stronger, fact-based counterarguments. After the role-play, switch roles and discuss the experience.

Did ya grab it? Are you annoyed by me yet?

7

HEALTHY HABITS

BOOSTING YOUR TEEN'S WELLNESS

You might be inclined to skip this chapter. You might be thinking, *I already know about healthy habits, healthy eating . . . blah, blah, blah.* However, I strongly recommend that you keep reading. In fact, you NEED to read this chapter, because like every other topic, this is an essential one that is going to help prepare your teen for life after high school and, honestly, will keep them around for WELL after high school years.

This chapter is dedicated to helping you in one of the most misunderstood areas of raising teens: health and wellness. When we teach this subject to teens in our programs, we break it up into these four pillars: Physical Health, Mental and Emotional Health, Nutrition, and Self-Care. All four are extremely important, and we'll touch on each throughout.

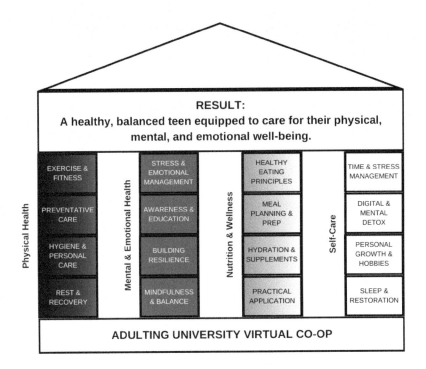

Alas, I only have one chapter to talk to you about this, so we are going to hone in on the one I believe is the most important for parents, especially in today's world, and that is the pillar of Mental and Emotional Health. After all, when teens are struggling with mental health, it can play a significant role in their daily life. It can negatively affect a teen's academic performance, social interactions, family relationships, motivation, personality, and more.

There is some overlap between emotional health and emotional intelligence, our topic from several chapters ago. However, for the goal of empowering you to really help your teen through what are often the most difficult years of a person's life, we're going to focus on the mental health side.

And here's the thing, I need to be VERY clear about this. I am NOT a psychologist. I am NOT a doctor. I am NOT a licensed therapist or counselor. I am a coach certified in youth mental health first aid and other trauma-informed care practices, and have worked with youth for more than 10 years of my career. It is important that you understand that what I am discussing is from experience and education, not licensing.

Before we get to the juicy stuff of how to really navigate this quite challenging area with your teen, we need to first understand what mental health is and the signs and symptoms to look out for, then we can get into what you can do to support your teen.

One last important disclaimer, if your teen is actively having thoughts of suicide or is harming themself, please seek professional help ASAP. The suicide hotline for teens in the United States is the **988 Suicide and Crisis Lifeline**. Teens (and anyone in crisis) can call or text **988** to be connected with a trained counselor who can provide support and assistance.

There is also **The Trevor Project** specifically for LGBTQ+ youth, which you can reach by calling **1-866-488-7386** or via text by texting "START" to **678-678**.

Both hotlines are available 24/7 and provide confidential support.

Okay, now that we've gotten through some of those details, let's get a better understanding of what youth mental health looks like right now in the world.

Block #1: Mental Health and Emotional Health

To help our teens overcome mental health challenges, or to get the help and support they need, we need to understand what is happening. Once we understand it, we can then learn to look for the signs and symptoms that show our teen is struggling or is trying to ask for help. And then we can give them the support they need.

In this section, we are going to go through that exact process together. And I want to give you a fair warning. This chapter will not be easy. It may ruffle your emotions. You might want to put the book down and stop reading. But please, stick it out. I promise it will be worth it in the end.

The Teen Mental Health Crisis

Mental health issues among teens have skyrocketed, especially since the COVID-19 pandemic. In fact (unpopular opinion), I believe that the teen/youth mental health crisis is the most under-reported and undervalued epidemic ever. It's essential that, as parents with kids, preteens, teens, and young adults, we understand and know what is going on with our youth around the world. This epidemic affects not just the United States—it is worldwide.

The stats and facts I'm about to share with you are heart wrenching. They are hard to read, hard to hear. This subject is something we don't want to think about. We don't want this to be our kid, but the sooner we can realize that our kids are not immune, and that we need to be proactive instead of reactive, then we significantly decrease the chances of our kids becoming a statistic.

Rising Feelings of Hopelessness

According to the Centers for Disease Control and Prevention (CDC), nearly 44% of high school students reported feeling persistently sad or hopeless in 2021, a significant increase from 28% in 2009. This sharp rise highlights the growing emotional struggles faced by our teens today (CDC).

Increasing Prevalence of Mental Health Disorders

The National Alliance on Mental Illness (NAMI) reports that one in six youth in the United States between the ages of 6 and 17 years experiences a mental health disorder annually. Alarmingly, despite this prevalence, only about 50% of these young individuals receive the treatment they need (NAMI).

Alarming Suicide Rates

Suicide rates among youth have been on the rise, marking suicide as one of the leading causes of death for individuals aged 10 to 24 years. The data reveals that more than 1.6 million young people have attempted suicide in recent years, reflecting the severe mental health crisis facing our youth (CDC).

These statistics may come as a surprise to parents who believe their teens are coping well. However, mental health issues, such as anxiety and depression, are becoming increasingly common among teens, often hidden behind smiles and good grades.

We never expect it to be our kid or our family member. AND it happens every day. After some of the most infamous suicides, families have claimed they didn't know. Or did they just not want to believe it? Hindsight is always 20/20, and when something tragic like that happens and we start to really look at it, we see that there were signs, red flags, and warnings, usually a lot of them.

I am telling you this from firsthand experience. I have lost several family members to suicide. The most impactful one for me was my uncle when I was 14 years old. He was one of my favorite people, always the funny, ornery uncle. I'll never forget it. We were at Cedar Point in Ohio on a family camping trip when my dad got the call. My dad is a very tough guy. He was in the military and has a very harsh exterior. He grew up in a rough family situation and lost his mom to an overdose when he was a kid. I remember my dad going outside our camper and seeing him crying. He was very close to his big brother, and that day broke him. He was never the same, and that event set a downward spiral in his life that eventually led to my parents' divorce.

Now, my uncle wasn't a teen—he was a grown man with a family. However, the impact, the loss, and the not knowing there was a problem were all the same.

A few years ago, I was helping our youth group at church. I was the leader of a group of amazing 8th grade girls. I had built some great relationships with these girls, and one day there was a tragedy in our district. An 8th grade boy at their school died by suicide in the middle of the street in front of his girlfriend's house with his parent's gun. It just so happened that this young man was good friends with most of the girls in my group. It was devastating seeing the ripple effect over all these lives that the young man had touched.

I know this topic is dark. It is depressing. It is so very sad. But there is hope. By being aware of the crisis that exists instead of pretending it isn't real, we can build a better path for our youth who are struggling.

Now that you know the reality your teen, your nieces and nephews, and your kids' friends all face, let's talk about how we can recognize those invisible warning flags to get support before things get too far.

Recognizing Signs and Symptoms

As a parent, knowing what to look for and see in identifying when someone is struggling with mental health is extremely important. And it is just as important to teach your teen to recognize signs and symptoms of mental health issues, such as depression, anxiety, and stress. It helps them be more cognizant and aware of not only their own feelings, emotions, and mental state, but those of their friends and family as well.

The most common types of mental health struggles we see in youth are anxiety and depression. In fact, here are some more statistics around these for you, and remember that these reflect only diagnosed cases. There are most likely double these numbers or even more that have gone undiagnosed.

Anxiety Disorders

Anxiety disorders are among the most common mental health issues in youth. These can include generalized anxiety disorder, social anxiety disorder, and panic disorder. Anxiety is more than just feeling nervous before a test. It can manifest as excessive worry, restlessness, difficulty concentrating, and even physical symptoms like headaches or stomachaches.

Think of anxiety like a broken smoke detector. It can go off even when there's no real danger.

According to the CDC, approximately 9.4% of children aged 3 to 17 years (about 5.8 million) have been diagnosed with anxiety (NAMI).

Depression

Depression is another prevalent mental health issue among youth, characterized by more than just feeling sad or down. Depression can manifest as a persistent feeling of sadness, hopelessness, or emptiness that doesn't go away. It often impacts a teen's daily functioning, affecting their ability to enjoy activities they once loved, maintain friendships, or even get out of bed in the morning. Symptoms can range from emotional signs like irritability, feelings of worthlessness, and difficulty concentrating to physical symptoms such as fatigue, changes in appetite, and sleep disturbances.

Think of depression like a heavy fog that settles in and clouds everything around it. It distorts a teen's perception of the world, making everything seem bleak and unmanageable, even when there's light and hope just beyond the mist. This fog isn't something that can just be "snapped out of." It requires support, understanding, and often professional help to clear away.

The CDC reports that 4.4% of children aged 3 to 17 years (about 2.7 million) have been diagnosed with depression (NAMI).

Many times, with our teens, the symptoms of these conditions can be subtle, meaning they may not always be super clear or easy to spot. Other times, the signs are there, but we as parents are oblivious because we don't know what to look for, or we may be in denial and not want to accept that our teen is struggling more than the average student.

Please hear me on this. And I am saying this with all the love I can muster, and you still may not love me because of it, in fact you may not like me anymore after this, but I want you to know that is okay, and I still like you no matter what!

Alright, please, if you suspect something, don't be afraid to talk to your teen or seek help. There is absolutely NO SHAME in seeking support and help for your teenager if you suspect they may be struggling with a mental health condition. It doesn't mean they are broken, and it doesn't mean they are any "less than" their peers. It just means there is something going on with the chemicals in their brain and they need help in this season.

Too many times I have seen parents not want to admit there may be something going on with their child, usually out of pride or embarrassment—neither of which is beneficial to their child. So please be on the lookout for the following signs that there may be something more serious going on than the average teen angst:

- *Behavioral Signs*:

  ○ Avoidance of Homeschool Activities and Family Responsibilities:

    • In a homeschool setting, a teen struggling with mental health might show reluctance to engage in daily lessons, projects, or family activities. They may procrastinate more than usual, avoid completing assignments, or express a desire to be left alone rather than participating in group learning or discussions. Example: If your teen frequently avoids taking part in their daily homeschool schedule, seems uninterested in family learning activities, or isolates themselves from group lessons, it could be a sign of underlying emotional distress or anxiety.

  ○ Withdrawal from Co-op or Extracurricular Activities:

    • Homeschooled teens often participate in co-ops, clubs, or community groups to socialize and learn with peers. A sudden disinterest in attending these activities or withdrawing from group interactions can signal depression or social anxiety. Example: Noticing your teen withdrawing from their homeschool co-op, avoiding club meetings, or refusing to join in on community activities they once enjoyed may show they are feeling overwhelmed or disconnected.

○ Increased Irritability or Conflicts at Home:

- Teens may become more irritable or easily angered during lessons or family interactions. They might have frequent arguments with siblings or display defiant behavior toward parents during homeschooling hours. Example: Frequent arguments with siblings or increased defiance during homeschooling sessions could suggest that your teen is dealing with frustration, stress, or other emotional challenges.

○ Focus on Perfectionism or Complete Loss of Motivation:

- A homeschool teen might either become excessively perfectionistic, obsessing over getting every detail right in their assignments, or they may show a complete lack of motivation, not wanting to start or complete any tasks. Example: If your teen focuses too much on achieving perfect results in every subject or, conversely, shows a lack of motivation to even begin their lessons, it might be a sign that they are struggling with anxiety or depression.

- *Emotional Signs*:

  ○ Persistent Sadness or Emotional Outbursts:

  - In a homeschooling environment, where parents and siblings are often around, a teen might show signs of persistent sadness, crying easily, or having emotional outbursts during lessons or daily activities. Example: If your teen seems to cry often or experiences emotional outbursts over minor frustrations during homeschooling, it could indicate they are feeling emotionally overwhelmed.

  ○ Feelings of Worthlessness or Hopelessness About Learning:

  - A teen might express feelings of worthlessness or hopelessness related to their homeschool work or their abilities. They might say things like "I'm not good at anything" or "What's the point of learning this?" Example: When a teen expresses doubt in their learning abilities or questions the value of their homeschooling education, it might be a sign of deeper emotional struggles.

- Lack of Interest in Family or Home Activities:

  - Emotional distress might cause a teen to lose interest in family activities, such as game nights, cooking together, or even informal educational outings they previously enjoyed. Example: A loss of interest in family activities or previously loved outings might suggest your teen is experiencing feelings of depression or anxiety.

- Difficulty Focusing on Lessons or Family Conversations:

  - A homeschooled teen struggling emotionally might find it hard to focus during lessons or when having conversations with family members. They may appear distracted, daydream, or frequently lose track of discussions. Example: If your teen often seems distracted during homeschool lessons or can't stay focused during family discussions, it could be a sign that they are dealing with internal emotional conflicts.

- *Physical Signs*:

  - Unexplained Aches and Pains During the Day:

    - In a homeschool environment, where parents are often more attuned to their child's daily habits, a teen might frequently complain about headaches, stomachaches, or other physical pains without a clear medical cause. Example: If your teen frequently complains about headaches or stomach pains, especially during homeschool hours or before engaging in activities, these could be physical signs of anxiety or stress.

  - Changes in Sleep Patterns Noticeable at Home:

    - As homeschool parents may notice their teen's sleeping habits more closely, changes such as sleeping too much, taking frequent naps, or struggling with insomnia could indicate mental health struggles. Example: If your teen starts sleeping more during the day or has trouble falling asleep at night, these changes in sleep patterns could be a behavioral indicator of depression or anxiety.

- ○ Decreased Energy and Enthusiasm for Physical Activities:

  - Homeschooled teens might show a lack of energy for activities they used to enjoy, such as outdoor play, sports, or even everyday chores around the house. Example: A noticeable decrease in energy or enthusiasm for daily physical activities, like outdoor play or helping with chores, might suggest that your teen is feeling fatigued because of emotional or psychological distress.

- ○ Frequent Fatigue Despite Adequate Rest:

  - Despite having the flexibility to rest as needed, a teen might still show signs of excessive fatigue or complain about feeling tired all the time, which can be a physical symptom of depression or anxiety. Example: Even with the ability to rest as needed, if your teen frequently complains of feeling tired or shows signs of fatigue, it could be a sign of underlying depression.

You might ask, "But Traci, a lot of these sound like my teen and their behavior. How am I supposed to know if it is just a typical teen thing or a warning sign?"

Great question, and here is my answer...

Think of it like this: It's normal for teens to have ups and downs, feel anxious about a big test, or be moody after a fight with a friend. But if you notice these behaviors happening more frequently, lasting longer, affecting their daily lives, or showing up without an obvious cause, it's worth looking closer. Pay attention to changes that seem out of character for your teen and persist. It's better to check in early and often than to wait and wonder.

Okay, now that we have spent some time really understanding some of the most common mental health struggles teens face, and the signs and symptoms to look for, let's now go to the next and final step, which is how you can help them.

How to Manage Mental Health

Here's the thing about mental health and teenagers. Not all teens have a full-blown mental health challenge that requires therapy and medication. Sometimes that is the case, but more times than not, they're struggling because they're not able to process their emotions, thoughts, or feelings in a healthy manner. We talked a lot about emotional management and regulation a few chapters ago, so I won't go too far into it here. However, what I want to talk about are three primary ways that students can better manage their mental health.

Healthy Coping Mechanisms

One of the biggest challenges we see with teens when they are struggling with mental health issues (and even adults too) is looking for a way to cope. And when they don't have healthy coping mechanisms or habits, that is when we see students turn to drugs, alcohol, or other things that put them in harm's way.

When our kids become overwhelmed, anxious, uncomfortable, and so on, it is so important that they have strategies they can turn to that will help them manage the stress, anxiety, and other emotions they're having in their day-to-day life.

There are many great techniques that can help your teen—it is just finding the one that works best for them. It could be meditation, physical activity, journaling, counseling, mentorship, listening to a specific playlist or podcast, watching a favorite movie, spending time with family... There really are so many options.

Mindfulness Techniques

When sharing about mindfulness, I don't just mean meditation and yoga. Although both can be great for calming your mind and body, I want to go deeper.

One of the absolute best ways to shift our mind to a more positive place is through gratitude. When we are practicing gratitude on a daily basis, it is very difficult for our mind to spiral and go to a negative place.

Another technique is to teach your teen how to express their emotions regularly. Putting your thoughts and feelings into words can help you reduce anxiety and frustration that you may be feeling.

Finally, encourage your teen to learn how to simplify their life. This means cutting out all the noise and things that are just mucking everything up. Help them establish what is important to them and what isn't, keeping only the things that matter most. This simplification helps provide clarity in our brains and reduces a lot of that stress, anxiety, and overwhelm we may be feeling.

Lifestyle Changes

Lifestyle changes can be tough for teens, especially when they are experiencing constant anxiety, depression, overwhelm, or stress. Incorporating such changes is what sometimes needs to happen for them to get to a better place. Here are a few ways your teen can implement healthy lifestyle changes.

Have a Morning Routine. Did you know the research shows that when we have a consistent morning routine, it sets our day up for success? In fact, John C. Maxwell says this: "You will never change your life until you change something you do daily. The secret of your success is found in your daily routine." Pretty powerful, huh? A study by Leaders.com found that 92% of highly successful people have a solid morning routine.

Now, let's be honest, this is easier said than done. However, if you can start small and then build, this can go a long way for your teen's mental health.

Make Sleep a Priority. Sleep is when our body repairs itself, when we become rejuvenated, and if we're not getting enough sleep, then our brain and body suffer. Help your teen find their ideal sleep schedule. Everyone is different, as some people need 6 hours, whereas others (like myself) need 8+ hours of sleep.

And it's not just about the amount but the timing. We all have our own inner timer or clock that functions the best when we go to bed at a specific time and wake up at a specific time EVERY day. Did you know each person has their own special sleep cycle to go through to get a well-rested night of sleep? That means that if your body needs to sleep from 10:30 pm to 7:30 am but you're not going to bed until 11:30 pm, then you actually could disrupt your sleep cycle and not hit all the stages like you're supposed to. Pretty crazy, right? Isn't science cool!? Sorry, nerd moment there...

Bottom line, sleep is important, and the RIGHT sleep schedule for each of us is even more important!!

Take Care of Your Physical Health. We all know the importance of healthy eating and exercise. Yet, most of us avoid it, especially when we're teenagers. And let's be honest, the last thing you want to do when you're feeling down or upset is eat your veggies (bring on the tub of ice cream, am I right?). That junk food and sugar might feel good in the moment, but it will not feel good later. And it certainly isn't giving our brain the nutrients it needs to function properly.

A great way to manage your mental health is through adopting healthy eating habits and getting some daily physical exercise. Devoting 30 minutes each day to physical activity can make an enormous difference. So, turn on some music, dance around the house, go for walks with your teen—find ways to be more active together and improve their health!

Supportive Relationships

The final piece of the puzzle in helping your teen with their mental health is supportive relationships. That means being the role model and modeling these healthy habits and coping strategies. It means having open communication and creating a safe environment for our teens to express themselves and their thoughts and feelings. And it means getting them the help and support they need.

The other aspect of supportive relationships extends beyond the home. At home is where it starts, but we also have to help our teens understand and know what they want in friendships and relationships they have outside of the home. Healthy relationships and friendships are a crucial piece to taking care of our mental health.

Conclusion

Helping your teen develop healthy habits is crucial for their overall well-being. By focusing on mental health, nutrition, physical activity, and self-care, you can guide them toward a balanced and fulfilling life. Remember, your guidance and support are key in helping them navigate the complexities of maintaining a healthy lifestyle.

So far, we've focused a lot on the soft skills and human side of preparing your teen for life after high school. Now, as we go into the next chapter, we are going to talk about some of the more practical life skills they need to succeed!

Put It Into Practice

Here are some activities that you can do with your teen to practice the things we discussed in this chapter and help your teen be on their way to taking care of their mental health!

1. JOINT ACTIVITY: Create a Stress Relief Toolkit Together

Work with your teen to create a physical or digital toolkit that includes items or practices they can use when feeling stressed or overwhelmed. This could include items like a stress ball, soothing music, a journal, or even a list of breathing exercises. Together, brainstorm what helps them feel better and compile everything into their personal "mental health toolkit."

2. SEPARATE ACTIVITY: Personal Journal Reflection

Encourage your teen to maintain a private journal where they can reflect on their emotions and coping mechanisms. Ask them to write about their feelings after experiencing a stressful event and how they dealt with it. Have them reflect on what worked, what didn't, and what they could do differently next time. Meanwhile, you can also take time to reflect on how you're supporting their mental health and track any progress or areas of concern.

3. TOGETHER EXERCISE: Practice Mindful Breathing

Set aside time each day to practice mindful breathing together. Sit down and go through a simple breathing exercise (e.g., inhale for 4 seconds, hold for 4 seconds, exhale for 4 seconds). This exercise is not only a great way for you to bond but also serves as a practical tool you both can use to manage stress. Afterward, talk about how it made you both feel and when it could be helpful to use.

4. ROLE-PLAY: Managing Stressful Situations

Role-play a scenario where your teen is feeling stressed or overwhelmed by schoolwork or social pressures. You'll take on the role of a calming influence, and your teen will practice using a coping mechanism (e.g., deep breathing or journaling) to navigate their feelings. Afterward, switch roles so that your teen can guide you through a stressful situation, encouraging the use of coping strategies.

So close to being done, please tell me you downloaded your workbook by now...

8

MONEY MATTERS

TEACHING YOUR TEEN THE BASICS

Let's talk about something that's a bit of a hot topic these days. This topic may have been off limits when you were growing up, like it was in my family, and because of that it has become this huge issue in today's families. What am I talking about you may ask? I'm talking about that green, the cheddar, the dough... I'm talking about money.

Financial literacy to be exact.

This topic is much more accepted in the homeschool world than in other places. However, it remains one of the most important topics to tackle. Statistics don't lie, and unfortunately, stats say that most people in the United States are living paycheck to paycheck, are up to their eyeballs in debt, and less than half of them have any money in retirement.

Basically, the upcoming generations from my millennial generation on down are going to be in trouble if things don't change on a very large scale. When I grew up, talking about money was a BIG no-no. My parents didn't talk about how much they made, how much the bills were, what the budget looked like, or what a budget was... I know I am not alone in this because for generations, talking about money was taboo. As if some crazy person would come rob them if people found out how much they made, like they had won the lottery or something.

And here's what happened: That lack of transparency has meant that financial literacy has not passed down to future generations. Now we have parents who are incapable of teaching their kids how to manage money successfully. Thank goodness for people like Dave Ramsey and Robert Kiyosaki who have started financial movements in our country, but we still have a long way to go!

Well, that changes today. We're going to talk about what your teen needs to know about money and how to teach it.

Understanding Financial Literacy

If you google "financial literacy," what comes up? For me, it is a definition by Investopedia that says, "Financial literacy is the ability to understand and effectively use various financial skills, including personal financial management, budgeting, and investing. When you are financially literate, you have the essential foundation for a smart relationship with money."

When we talk about financial literacy, there are so many parts and pieces. Literacy isn't just managing your money, it isn't just knowing how to budget and live within your means. It is also understanding how banking works, how credit works, how debt works, and its impact. It is understanding the different ways to buy a home or a car. Knowing how insurance works and what is essential and what isn't. It is knowing the different ways to prepare for your future and leave a legacy for future generations.

And as a parent, teaching all these may seem very overwhelming. Where do you even start? Well, just like in our other chapters, we have a system for this! In fact, when we teach our financial literacy course to teens, we cover the entire topic from foundations to advanced concepts.

We have provided a graphic of our four foundational pillars of personal finance and the blocks that make them up. They include Financial Foundations, Saving and Debt, Next-Level Money Management, and Future Planning.

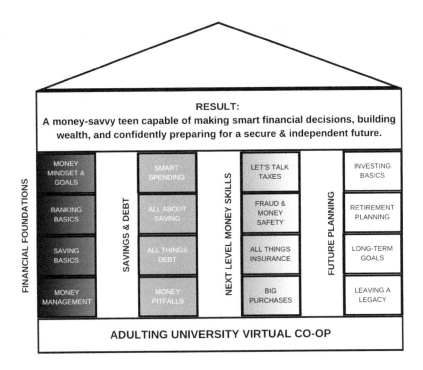

For this chapter, we are going to focus on the first pillar: Financial Foundations. Specifically, we're going to look at our first block, which is Money Mindset and Goals.

Block #1: Money Mindset and Goals

So you might ask, "Why would you teach me about money mindset and goals and not banking basics or money management?" That is a brilliant question! And here's why...

You could learn all the "right" ways to manage your money, understand the financial system inside and out, know how to invest, and do all the right things, and STILL make poor financial decisions and end up living paycheck to paycheck. Why? Because if your mindset around money isn't right, then none of the rest matters.

Mindset is everything. I've known people living paycheck to paycheck making $40,000 a year, and I've known people living paycheck to paycheck making more than $250,000 a year. If your mindset isn't right around money, then no matter how much you make, it'll never be "enough."

What Is Mindset?

There are several money mindsets, but I want to focus on the top three: scarcity/fixed, abundance, and avoidance/growth. Let's look at what each of these looks like...

Scarcity/Fixed Mindset

People with a scarcity or fixed mindset believe that money is limited and that their financial situation is difficult or impossible to change. This mindset can lead to stress, fear of taking financial risks, and missed opportunities for growth. Those with this mindset may avoid investing or pursuing financial education because they believe their current situation is set in stone, creating a cycle of financial insecurity.

For example, someone might say, "I'll never make enough money to get ahead, so why bother trying?" They may focus on saving as much as possible but shy away from opportunities to grow their wealth.

Avoidance Mindset

The avoidance mindset is characterized by ignoring or neglecting financial responsibilities because dealing with money causes discomfort or anxiety. This can lead to unintentional debt accumulation, missed payments, and lack of financial planning. Individuals with this mindset might avoid budgeting, ignore financial statements, or delay making important financial decisions.

For example, a teen might refuse to create a budget or avoid talking about their finances because they find it stressful, which could lead to accumulating unnecessary debt later in life.

Abundance/Growth Mindset

Those with an abundance/growth mindset believe that money is plentiful and that they have the power to improve their financial situation through learning, effort, and strategic decision making. This mindset encourages optimism, calculated risk taking, and long-term financial planning. People with this mindset are more likely to invest in their education and actively seek opportunities to grow their wealth and achieve financial goals.

For example, a teen with an abundance/growth mindset might take on a part-time job to save for a goal while also learning about investing and personal finance to ensure long-term success.

It is important to define our mindset around money. The goal is to have an abundance/growth mindset, as this helps us see money positively and make smart financial decisions.

What Creates Our Money Mindset

Before we can talk about how to shift our current money mindset to one with a more positive flair, we need to understand what influenced and created our current mindset around money. Typically, there are several factors that form our money mindset, such as the environment we are raised in, the surrounding culture, and our money personality. These are what we call the *psychology of money*.

Our Environment

Our environment is one of the biggest factors shaping how we view money, and simply this is how you, as the parent, have viewed money, talked about money, and used money in your home. Just like we've talked about a lot so far in this book, kids learn through seeing how you do things. Even if we don't think so, our teens are watching us closely, and they have been since we were born. The worst part about this is that they will often emulate the same things you're doing without even realizing it. It's the concept that more things are caught than taught. This takes being a money role model to the next level, doesn't it?

Some environmental factors that influence our money mindset (and our kids) include things like this:

- How our parents talked about money (if they did)

- If they avoided talking about money (like mine)

- Spending habits (cash, credit cards, buying all the things, not spending money, etc.)

- Any fights or arguments about money (one of the top reasons for divorce)

- The primary feelings at home about money (stress, peace, etc.)

Now, you might beat yourself up right now about this, but stop right there. We all have messed up with money and parenting. It is never too late to change our own mindset and habits around money and lead by example. And I'm going to give you some ways to do this in just a few more paragraphs!

Our Culture

The culture in which we grow up can play a big part in forming our money mindset. What follows are several ways that culture affects how we view and handle finances.

Cultural Norms and Beliefs. Every culture has its own set of values and norms about money, wealth, and success. In some cultures, financial success might be seen as the highest form of achievement, whereas in others, modesty and saving might be emphasized over outward displays of wealth.

For example, in many Western cultures, personal success is often associated with material wealth and status. In contrast, in more collectivist cultures, like in some parts of Asia, families prioritize saving, financial security, and providing for the family.

Religious and Ethical Teachings. In some cultures, religious and ethical teachings include guidelines or beliefs about how to handle money. Some religions promote the idea that one should use money to help others, leading to charitable giving, whereas others may view wealth as a sign of divine favor.

For example, in Christianity, the Bible encourages stewardship of money and resources, teaching that we should manage wealth responsibly and share with those in need.

Economic Conditions and Historical Context. A society's historical and economic experiences also shape cultural perspectives on money. In countries that have experienced economic instability, war, or hyperinflation, people may develop a scarcity mindset, always fearing financial hardship or preparing for the worst.

For example, in countries like Venezuela, where there has been significant economic turmoil, families may teach their children to hoard cash or mistrust banks.

Media and Cultural Messaging. Media plays a powerful role in shaping cultural attitudes toward money. Films, TV shows, and social media often portray specific ideals about wealth and success, which can influence a society's collective money mindset.

For example, in Western media, celebrities and influencers often flaunt luxury lifestyles, which can promote a status-oriented mindset where people view accumulating wealth as a way to gain social capital.

Our Money Personality

Finally, another large factor is our own personality. There are multiple personalities around money, based on what we call *money tendencies*. All of us have personalities, and our personalities help us make decisions, act a certain way, and say certain things. It is no different with our money. One way to identify our money mindset is to know what our money personality is.

The most common money tendencies/personalities are spender vs. saver, nerd vs. free spirit, and safety vs. status.

Spender vs. Saver. This one is usually pretty easy to identify. Are you someone who enjoys spending money or saving it? If your teen is the type of person who gets a little money and MUST go shopping or to Starbucks right then and there, they're probably a spender.

Or maybe your teen is someone who has a hard time buying things for themselves, and often wants to save and be patient. If that is them, then they are likely a saver.

Both types have strengths and weaknesses. Spenders often are very generous, and savers can be patient and frivolous with money. However, it is when we become extreme in either direction that things can get tricky.

Nerd vs. Free Spirit. You will probably know where you and your teen fall in this one too. Nerds are the "detail" people. They love the numbers—budgeting and managing money come naturally to them. They want to know everything and are very organized.

Free spirits are the opposite. They don't like to get into the nitty-gritty. Details overwhelm them and make them uncomfortable. They like to live life to the fullest and just enjoy moments.

Again, both tendencies have strengths, but it is also important that our nerds learn how to loosen up a bit sometimes and have fun, and that our free spirits learn how the details can be important, especially with money.

Safety vs. Status. Finally, we have safety versus status. This one is often deeply rooted in our views and insecurities and isn't always easy to see. Our instincts for safety and status produce deeply held motivations and really drive how we view and use money.

Those financially motivated by safety want financial security. They don't want to be living paycheck to paycheck. They don't want to be worried about money and often can find themselves quite stressed about money when their safety is at risk. If not careful, this motivation can cause them to live in constant fear and worry, always wondering if they'll stay safe.

Those motivated by status dress to impress. They have an inner desire to look successful, like they have it all together. These individuals lean toward a "keeping up with the Joneses" mentality, where it is all about the best and nicest things. This motivation can keep them broke and in debt just to look rich. It is okay to want nice things, but we can't let that desire lead us to become materialistic.

I want you to take a minute and absorb everything you just read, then ask yourself these questions:

- How do I view money?

- What is my money personality?

- Do I go a little too extreme in either direction?

- How did my family talk about money when I was growing up?

It is important to know where we are with our own money mindset before we can help our teens.

Creating a Healthy Money Mindset

Now, let's talk about how we can shift our teen's mindset to a growth and abundance view around money. Here are seven steps to create a healthy mindset around money.

Step #1: Know and Understand Your Beliefs About Money. Start by discussing family beliefs about money with your teen. Ask them what they think about saving, spending, and earning. Help them understand that the first step in creating a healthy mindset is recognizing their current beliefs and where they come from.

Step #2: Read Influential Books to Shape Your Mindset. Encourage your teen to read books that can help them see money differently. Books like *Rich Dad Poor Dad* by Richard Kiyosaki or *The Total Money Makeover* by Dave Ramsey can offer a fresh perspective and help teens understand how wealth building really works.

Step #3: Give Away Money. Teach your teen the value of generosity. Show them how giving, whether it's through donating or helping a friend in need, can shift their focus from scarcity to abundance. It's not about the amount but the habit of sharing.

Step #4: Dream About the Possibilities. Sit down with your teen and talk about their financial dreams—whether it's saving for a car or funding a passion project. Encourage them to dream big, as it helps them see the possibilities that come with financial success.

Step #5: Believe in the Possibilities. Help your teen build confidence in their ability to achieve financial goals. Talk about examples of people who turned small steps into big success stories. Reinforce that with the right mindset, anything is achievable.

Step #6: Commit to the Change. Help your teen create healthy financial habits that they stick to, whether it's saving a portion of their allowance or budgeting their spending. The key is consistency.

Step #7: Practice Gratitude. Teach your teen to appreciate what they already have. Practicing gratitude can shift their focus from "I need more" to "I have enough," which helps create a positive relationship with money.

Now that we have a solid understanding about mindset, let's talk about the other important foundational piece in this block: money goals.

What Are Financial Goals?

Once you create a positive mindset around money, the next foundational step is to create financial or money goals. This motivates us to keep pushing forward, to say no to things that don't align, to stay the tough course of good financial stewardship.

When we talk about money goals, these can be short-term goals like saving up for a new video game or long-term goals like buying a car or a home. It is important that we teach our teens how to set financial goals for different areas of their lives, not just retirement, housing, or transportation. And the more specific goals they create, the better.

In fact, let's talk about the best way to create money goals, and that is using what is called the *SMART Goal Method.* Now, you may have heard of this before. It is such a common framework that many people tune out when they hear it. Please don't do that, even if you have heard this term a million times and it feels like beating a dead horse. This framework has proven to be the most effective way to not only set goals but also achieve them.

Creating SMART Financial Goals

Before we can create money goals in a SMART format, we first need to understand what it means.

Specific. Help your teen define exactly what they want to achieve. Instead of vague goals like "save money," encourage them to be specific, such as "save $500 for a new laptop." This clarity helps your teen stay focused and motivated.

Measurable. Ensure the goal is measurable so you can track progress. For instance, if the goal is to save $500, parents can guide their teen to break that into smaller milestones—like saving $50 a month. This keeps the goal tangible and gives a clear way to track success.

Achievable. Make sure the goal is realistic and attainable. Encourage your teen to set a financial goal that they can achieve based on their allowance, part-time job income, or other sources of money. This helps avoid frustration while building confidence as they reach their targets.

Relevant. The goal should relate directly to their life. Teach your teen to choose financial goals that align with their personal interests or needs. For example, saving for a laptop to help with homeschooling or setting aside money for a summer trip will resonate more strongly with them than abstract financial goals.

Time-bound. Set a clear deadline for achieving the goal. This adds urgency and helps teens stay focused. For example, they could aim to save $500 by the end of 6 months. Having a time frame will motivate them to manage their money consistently.

The reason this method is so effective isn't just because we are putting goals down on paper, it is because we are laying out the actual plan for how and when we are going to achieve this goal when we create it.

A goal without a plan is just a wish. And this method takes our "wish" and makes it a reality we can actually achieve. This is also a great motivator for your teen, who may be a little "whatever" about learning good money management. Having them dream about what they want and then putting it into this format makes it more real and achievable, meaning it is a good motivator to do what is necessary to make it happen.

Think about this for a second. Has your teen ever really wanted something? Like I mean REALLY, REALLY wanted something, and they were willing to do whatever it took to make it happen? Like clean the bathrooms, bring you breakfast in bed, or clean up the dog poop in the yard?

I know when our son really wants something, he turns into this angel of a child doing all the right things to try to "earn" whatever it is he wants. I mean, when he wants his friends over for a sleepover and the deal is that he has to do his chores first, he suddenly turns into the most efficient cleaner I have ever seen and gets all his chores done in a day instead of dragging it out through the entire week.

It is amazing what a motivator things can be when you really want them. And it is no different with goal setting and managing your money. It all depends on how badly you want it.

People who go all in on Dave Ramsey's methods and "Gazelle Intensity" are at the point where they want nothing more than to be out of debt. They're sick and tired of being broke, and are ready to do the work to make it happen.

We have to find that motivation within our teens and then show them they can make it happen if they do x, y, and z.

Let's look at a few SMART money goal examples that are good motivators for teens:

The Musician

- Specific: "I want to save $300 for a new guitar."

- Measurable: "I'll save $30 a week from my part-time job."

- Achievable: "Based on my weekly allowance and job, I can save this amount."

- Relevant: "I love playing music, and a new guitar will help me improve."

- Time-bound: "I'll reach this goal in 10 weeks."

The Gamer

- Specific: "I want to save $400 to buy the latest gaming system."

- Measurable: "I'll set aside $40 from my weekly allowance and odd jobs."

- Achievable: "With my weekly income, I can save this much over this period."

- Relevant: "I'm passionate about gaming, and this system will let me play with friends online."

- Time-bound: "I'll reach my savings goal in 10 weeks."

The New Driver

- Specific: "I want to save $2,000 for a down payment on my first car."

- Measurable: "I'll save $200 a month from my part-time job."

- Achievable: "I can realistically set aside $200 per month with my job and allowance."

- Relevant: "This car will give me more freedom to get to activities and part-time work."

- Time-bound: "I'll achieve this goal in 10 months."

The College Bound
- Specific: "I want to save $1,000 for my first year of college expenses."

- Measurable: "I'll contribute $100 a month from my job and birthday money."

- Achievable: "Based on my current part-time job, I can save this amount each month."

- Relevant: "Saving for college will help me be prepared for tuition or supplies."

- Time-bound: "I'll hit my goal by the time I graduate in 10 months."

The Newest Tech
- Specific: "I want to save $800 for a new phone."

- Measurable: "I'll save $50 from my weekly babysitting jobs and tutoring."

- Achievable: "I can set aside $50 per week, which makes this goal realistic."

- Relevant: "This phone will help me stay connected with family, friends, and school."

- Time-bound: "I'll save enough in 16 weeks."

Now that we've learned how we can teach our teen how to create money goals they actually want to achieve, let's look at the last piece of the goal-making puzzle, which increases our chance of success.

Transforming Goals Into Reality

SMART goals are the first step toward achieving the things we want. Next, we present a few other things that we need to do, and our teens need to do, to give us the highest probability of success.

Write Goals Down and Refer to Them Regularly. Research shows that people who write down their goals are significantly more likely to achieve them. Encourage your teen to write down their SMART goals and keep them visible—whether in a journal, on a whiteboard, or as a phone reminder. The act of writing makes the goal tangible, and referring to it frequently keeps it top of mind, boosting commitment.

Break Down Larger Goals Into Smaller Milestones. After setting the SMART goal, break it down into smaller, manageable steps. This helps maintain focus and momentum. For example, if the goal is to save $1,000 for a new laptop, break it down into monthly or weekly savings targets. This creates quick wins and prevents the goal from feeling overwhelming.

Track Progress Regularly. Successful people regularly check in on their progress. Encourage your teen to track their financial goals either in a notebook, a goal-setting app, or even a spreadsheet. Seeing incremental progress helps maintain motivation and allows them to adjust if they're falling behind

Celebrate Small Wins. Celebrating milestones keeps motivation high. Parents can encourage teens to celebrate hitting smaller savings goals (e.g., "You saved your first $100! Let's do something fun to celebrate!"). These small rewards provide motivation to keep going.

Stay Accountable. Accountability plays a significant role in goal achievement. Encourage your teen to share their goal with a family member or friend who can help keep them on track. Parents can also be accountability partners by checking in regularly to discuss progress and challenges.

Visualize Success. Visualization is a powerful tool. Encourage teens to create a vision board or mental image of what achieving their financial goal will look like. For instance, have them visualize what it'll feel like to purchase that new gaming system or take that road trip with the car they're saving for. This keeps the end goal exciting and tangible.

Adjust When Necessary. Life can throw curveballs, so flexibility is key. Teach teens that it's okay to adjust their SMART goals when needed. Whether it's because of unexpected expenses or changes in income, adjusting the timeline or milestones can keep them on track without feeling discouraged.

Financial or money goals are so important for lifelong success. After all, the most successful people in the world are goal setters and achievers. It is what keeps them focused, driven, and moving forward. It is that inner motivation that we bring to the surface and put words and a plan behind. And every teen needs this skill to be well on their way to success!

Conclusion

Learning effective money management skills is truly an essential skill that every teen should know before they leave school. However, this foundational skill of money mindset and money goals is a crucial first step that gets them in the right mindset and framework to actually value learning the other skills around money management.

This isn't something that happens overnight. Changing your mindset around money and goals involves repetition, consistency, support, and encouragement. So, keep going mama! You're doing a great job, and before you know it, your teen will be on their way to having a mindset of abundance and growth, which makes the learning process and journey so much easier!

Put It Into Practice

Here are some activities that you can do with your teen to practice the things we discussed in this chapter and help your teen be well on their way to being masters of their money!

1. JOINT ACTIVITY: Create a Vision Board for Financial Goals

Work together to create a financial vision board using magazines, printouts, or drawings. Both mom and teen can add images that represent their financial goals, such as a new car, vacation, or savings targets. Discuss each other's goals as you build the board, talking about the mindset needed to achieve them and how they can become SMART goals.

2. SEPARATE ACTIVITY: Journal on Money Beliefs

Ask your teen to reflect on their personal beliefs about money. Have them journal about questions like "What does money mean to me?" and "What do I believe is possible for me financially?" While they are journaling, you can also reflect on your own money beliefs to compare later. Afterward, have an open conversation about how each of you sees money, discussing similarities and differences in your mindsets.

3. TOGETHER EXERCISE: Create a Budget for a Shared Goal

Work together on setting a shared financial goal, like saving for a family trip or purchasing something that benefits both of you. Create a budget together, calculate how much to save, and decide on what changes or sacrifices are necessary to achieve the goal. This exercise reinforces the importance of financial planning while working toward a common objective.

4. ROLE-PLAY: Navigate a Purchase Decision

Create a role-play scenario where your teen wants to buy something expensive, like the latest gaming console, and you, as the parent, are questioning the purchase. Practice discussing financial goals, money mindset, and the reasons behind wanting the purchase. Then switch roles where your teen plays the parent questioning the decision and you play the teen. This encourages both of you to think critically about spending, saving, and prioritizing financial goals.

Well... Technically you can still grab the workbook here...

9

EMPOWERING INDEPENDENCE
RAISING SELF-SUFFICIENT TEENS

L et me ask you a question... Do you want your teen to still be living with you when they're 30 or 40? Hopefully, your response is a giant "Heck no! I want them to be on their own, to have a family. I want to be looking forward to grandchildren, not taking care of a grown man/woman child."

In today's world, we are seeing a HUGE amount of young adults moving back home after leaving the nest, going through one failure after another, falling flat on their face and ending up back home OR never leaving to begin with! Why is this happening?

Well, here is my opinion, backed by research and experience, mind you. The world is a hot mess, but that isn't the root problem. We are seeing teens waiting longer to get driver's licenses, not wanting to leave home, not wanting to take on responsibilities and independence. And here is my probably unpopular opinion: Young adults aren't leaving home because there is no reason to.

What do I mean by that? Well, when your parents are taking care of you even after you're 18, doing your laundry, cleaning up after you, giving you allowance, putting you in a comfort zone bubble with no challenges, no responsibilities, no motivation to leave, then why would you ever want to leave?

Unfortunately, this has become the norm. I see it every day in the 50+ parent groups I'm part of. Parents with older teens or young adults complaining about the disrespect their kids give them, how they do nothing for themselves, how they have no motivation to do anything other than hang out with their friends and play video games.

Students going to college, getting a degree, then moving back home to "find a job and save money" but not actually doing that. Or students graduating high school, not going to college, not going to work, not going to a trade program, just lost, working at McDonald's with no ambitions, no motivation to do anything different.

Now, you might find an excuse like "Well this is my child, but they don't live at home because they haven't learned responsibility or independence," or you may feel they're still there just because they have had a hard time or they have mental health struggles or they are just comfortable there. I've even heard moms say, "I would be happy if my kid wanted to live here with me forever and never move out."

Well, I hate to be the bearer of bad news or disappointment, but this is not the best for your child. This approach of keeping your kids with you, allowing them to always come home and to feel like they can just come back and have no responsibilities is setting our kids up for failure. And not the good kind of failure. I'm talking about life altering, mind-wrecking, spiraling failure.

When our teens and young adults have no desire to leave home, have no desire to do things on their own, have no desire to grow up, we end up with an entire generation of entitled and dependent young adults. Some of you might like that your kids are dependent because makes you feel loved, valued, and like your kids will always "need" you. However, what this actually means is that when you're no longer around, your full-grown adult will not only have lost their mom or dad and primary caregiver, but they also are going to crash and burn. And no parent wants that for their kids, because we love our children.

The first thing we as parents have to do if we are holding our kids back from independence is to identify why. Why don't we want our kids to grow up and leave home? Why aren't we letting our kids learn how to function without us?

Once we identify these motivators, we can work on them and then transition to help our teens prepare for a life of independence. It doesn't mean they won't still "need" you, because we always "need" our parents. It just becomes a different kind of need than it was when we were little kids who relied on our parents for everything, including survival.

In fact, when we prepare our kids for life without us, we actually create a stronger, deeper bond than we ever could by keeping them dependent and irresponsible.

And I know these things come from a place of love. We love and want to protect our kids, so we like to put them in bubbles. We don't want them to experience struggles or difficulty or feel overwhelmed. But that is part of life, and when we can let our kids experience this when they are still home as teens, when they're safe, they are going to go so much further in life than their counterparts who have not had these experiences.

Foundations of Independence

We have four foundational blocks of what we call independence or independent living: Personal Responsibility and Accountability, Independence and Self-Sufficiency, Home Management, and Self-Management. These blocks are truly essential to raising a young adult who is ready to take on life and be able to not just survive but thrive on their own.

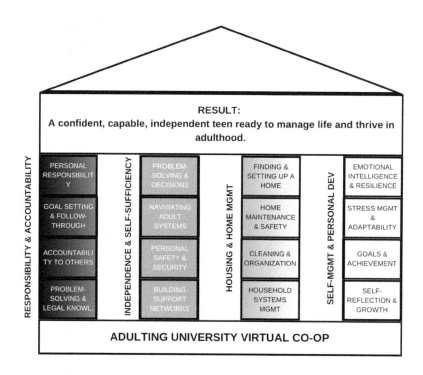

Here's why we go through the blocks in that particular order when teaching the foundations of independence to teens...

Starting with responsibility and accountability is like laying the foundation for a house—you can't build the rest without it! Teens need to know how to manage their own time, own up to their decisions, and take charge of their actions. Once they've got this down, they're ready to tackle bigger, more adult-sized responsibilities.

Now that they've learned the basics of owning their choices, it's time to step up. Independence and self-sufficiency mean becoming comfortable with solving their own problems, handling adult systems (think banks and bills), and relying less on mom and dad. These skills are their toolkit for managing life on their own.

After mastering self-reliance, teens are ready to dive into the practical stuff—like finding and managing a home, understanding how utilities work, and creating a safe space for themselves. It's about learning the nitty-gritty of adulting so they can thrive, not just survive.

This is where long-term success happens. After they've learned the ropes, teens need to continue growing—emotionally, mentally, and physically. It's about self-care, stress management, and setting goals that keep them on track for personal success. Independence isn't just about surviving—it's about thriving and evolving.

For the rest of this chapter, we are going to focus specifically on the first block.

Block #1: Personal Responsibility and Accountability

In a homeschooling environment, personal responsibility means that teens are taking ownership of their learning, daily tasks, and decisions. It's about knowing that their actions, like completing assignments or meeting deadlines, are their own responsibility, and they influence the outcome.

Accountability goes hand in hand with this—it's about recognizing when they've made a mistake, owning it, and learning from it. It's also about being answerable to others, whether that's their parents, teachers, or even themselves, for the commitments they've made.

Teaching teens responsibility and accountability early on is like handing them the keys to their future. These traits are foundational to their success in life, influencing everything from school performance to relationships.

When teens learn how to be responsible for their actions and hold themselves accountable, they develop a stronger work ethic and a sense of independence. This helps them transition into adulthood, where they'll need to manage their own homes, careers, finances, and interactions with others.

Reliable adults rest on a foundation of accountability—they become trusted employees, responsible partners, and people who can navigate life's ups and downs with resilience and integrity.

Let's be real—teaching responsibility isn't always easy. Teens naturally push back against authority, and they might resist owning up to their mistakes. Sometimes they make excuses or blame others to avoid taking responsibility.

And as a homeschooling mom, you might often find yourself in the tricky position of balancing the roles of both teacher and parent, which can make enforcing accountability even harder. The good news is that these challenges are normal, and there are strategies to help your teen embrace responsibility, which we're going to explore together now!

Next, I'm sharing four strategies and tools that you can start using today to empower your teen to be well on their way to being a responsible and accountable adult.

Personal Responsibility

Up first is personal responsibility, which simply means having your teen understand and own their actions, choices, and consequences (both good and bad). This means they need to develop self-discipline and skills that give them the opportunity to take charge of their own actions, and own up to their mistakes without playing the blame game.

Here are two ways you can help your teen develop this skill.

Model It at Home

Are you tired of hearing this yet? I wouldn't blame you if you are. You wouldn't be too far off if you told people that the core lesson of this book is to act the way we want our teens to act.

With these skills, especially soft skills, our kids are often a reflection of how we show up in the world and at home. That saying about toddlers, "They're like sponges and just absorb everything they see and hear," doesn't go away as they get older. It just isn't quite as noticeable.

This can be a hard pill to swallow, especially as a mom. We want our little angels to grow up and do all the right things and be amazing people. We don't want our kids to be the apple that didn't fall too far from the tree.

But here's the good news. If we can model these behaviors, it will slowly wear off on our teens. We can literally teach them the better way of doing things without nagging, without lecturing, without saying a word. After all, actions speak louder than words. (Wow, a lot of idioms and proverbs in this chapter, sorry y'all!)

If we want our teens to take responsibility, then we have to lead by example. That means being consistent, managing our time, showing up for commitments and keeping our word, and sometimes the hardest thing—admitting when we make mistakes and apologizing (buh-bye pride).

A great way to do this at home is to have conversations with your teen about some of those grown-up responsibilities like paying bills, managing a schedule, making appointments, and sharing with them when you've made mistakes and what you learned from them.

Set Clear Expectations

The second way to teach responsibility is to set clear expectations. Let's be honest, we all do so much better when we know what others expect of us. Teens are no different. In fact, it is even more important for them to have clear guidelines and expectations so that they know where the bar is.

Could you imagine trying to do a sport like high-jump or pole vault without the bar that measures how far you are supposed to jump? It would be a joke. Nobody would know if they beat their own personal record, if they qualified for the next round, or if they broke a world record.

And even worse, could you imagine if the ref knew where it was supposed to be? They went up a ladder ahead of time and marked a black dot at the spot where people were expected to jump, but then they didn't tell anyone or provide them with the actual bar to jump with!? It would be a disaster of an event.

It is no different for our teens. When they don't know where the bar is, they don't know what they're aiming for, and then if they fall short, or when they get in trouble or fail, now they're frustrated, angry, hurt, and feel like they were lied to, taken advantage of, or set up to fail. And by their OWN parents! Not ideal for a healthy relationship.

So make sure that you set clear expectations with your teen, whether it is for their schoolwork, chores, or other commitments and responsibilities. A great way to do this is to write them down and put them in a place that is visible to them. This could be a responsibility chart that includes that week's expectations around chores, assignments, and more!

Check in with them and keep them up-to-date on any changes to the expectations, and have conversations often about what those expectations are BEFORE they need them.

Goal Setting and Follow-Through

The next area that is so important for independence is goal setting and follow-through. This is a great way for teens to learn both responsibility and accountability by helping them learn how to set their own goals and expectations and create the plan that is going to help them achieve them.

Let's look at two ways to teach your teens goal setting and follow-through.

The SMART Goal Method

We talked in depth about SMART goals in the previous chapter. Just to refresh, a SMART goal has the following characteristics:

- Specific

- Measurable

- Achievable

- Relevant

- Time-bound

For example, if your teen wanted to buy the newest video game, or pair of Jordans, a SMART goal could be something like this:

- *Specific*: "I want to buy the newest video game, which costs $60."

- *Measurable*: "I will save $60 by putting aside $10 from my weekly allowance or earnings each week."

- *Achievable*: "I will complete extra chores and limit unnecessary spending to ensure I have $10 each week to save."

- *Relevant*: "Buying this game is important to me because it's something I've been looking forward to, and I'll use it to play with my friends."

- *Time-bound*: "I will save the full $60 and buy the game in 6 weeks."

By using this model, the plan is now built right into the goal. This provides more structure for your teen and makes follow-through so much easier. It also gets teens more excited about their dreams and goals by forming them into a framework that makes it feel much more like a reality, and less like something they could never accomplish.

Choices and Consequences

The other part of this goal setting and follow-through is providing the opportunity for your teen to make choices on their own, and to experience consequences, good or bad, that can come from their choices.

That's right mama, I'm encouraging you to let your teen experience natural consequences that can happen when we don't follow through on things, or when we make poor choices.

I know, it can be hard. Remember, we want to put our kid in a bubble and never experience pain, suffering, failure... And if they don't get to experience these things in the safety of your home, they will experience them in the real world, which isn't always as kind.

Giving teens the power to make decisions builds responsibility.

An easy way to ease them into this is to let them choose how to structure their day or when to complete tasks, but ensure they understand that choices come with consequences, both good and bad. And if we set a clear expectation of what those consequences are, it won't be a surprise when it happens.

For example, you can let them decide when they are going to do their chores or schoolwork. You could say, "You can decide when you want to get this assignment/chore completed. However, the expectation/requirement is that if it isn't done by 6:00 pm tonight, then you lose your phone all day tomorrow and will have to go do it right then regardless of what you are doing. If you get it done by that time, then you earn an extra 30 minutes of gaming time tomorrow."

In the example, you've set clear expectations of what they need to do and by when. They know both the good and bad consequences of their actions. Now, it is up to them to be responsible and get their work done by the deadline. If they don't, then they already know the consequences and won't be surprised when you say, "Well it is after 6:00 pm and your work isn't done, so I'm going to have you stop playing your game right now and put your phone on lockdown. Go get it done right now, please. Thank you."

The situation becomes very matter of fact, with no need for yelling or arguing. Your teen will experience a natural consequence of their choices. This encourages teens to be more responsible, stick to the expectations, and improve their follow-through on what they've set out to achieve.

Accountability to Others

Next up is the idea of accountability to others, not just themselves. Think of this as them recognizing their responsibilities in relationships, teams, and family. It helps them fulfill obligations and commitments they've made to others with integrity and reliability.

Some ways you can teach your teen this idea of accountability are shared next.

Encouraging Family Teamwork

Especially as homeschoolers, it is important to learn collaboration, teamwork, and following through on commitments. That is what accountability is all about. A great way to do this is to have your teen get involved in family projects where everyone is contributing something.

This takes some of the pressure off your teen feeling like they are the only one who has responsibility in a situation. Instead, it shows them that everyone has something to contribute and is bringing value to the group. It also can open the door to conversations about what happens when one person in the group doesn't pull their weight, and what those consequences are for the rest of the team.

Here are some fun ways to promote teamwork:

- *Meal Planning and Cooking Together*: Involve the whole family in planning a weekly menu, shopping for ingredients, and preparing meals. Assign roles like choosing the recipes, chopping vegetables, or setting the table.

- *Family Field Trip Planner*: Rotate the responsibility of planning a monthly family field trip. One family member or a small group can take charge of researching, selecting, and organizing the trip, including transportation, budgeting, and activities.

- *DIY Home Project*: Work together on a home improvement or craft project, such as painting a room, building a bookshelf, or creating homemade decorations.

- *Game Night Challenge*: Create a family game night where each family member picks and teaches the group their favorite game. Everyone collaborates to set up, explain rules, and play.

- *Family Business Venture*: Set up a small family-run business, like a lemonade stand, bake sale, or selling handmade crafts. Assign roles based on strengths, such as marketing, accounting, or customer service.

- *Story Writing Relay*: Each family member contributes a section to a collaborative story, building on each other's ideas. Once complete, illustrate the story as a team.

- *Home Science Fair*: Work together on science experiments, where each family member leads one project and involves others in conducting the experiments.

One of the best ways to teach accountability is showing the value you have and the value your word has for others. When we don't carry our end of the bargain, it affects the people who were relying on us at that moment.

Create a Contract

Another great way to teach accountability is to create a contract. Having a written agreement of what the expectations are with chores, study schedules, or commitments and what the consequences are if we don't hold up our end can be a powerful way to teach our teens accountability.

A contract or agreement that we physically see and sign reinforces the importance of keeping promises and fulfilling expectations that others have of us. It becomes a tangible reminder of what's expected and can be referred to if necessary.

When creating these agreements or contracts, make it a collaborative effort where your teen helps set their own goals and tasks. This increases buy-in and accountability.

Here are some great examples of contracts to create for your teen:

- Driving contract

- Chore responsibility contract

- Curfew contract

- Technology and screen time contract

- Allowance or budgeting contract

Problem Solving and Adaptability

The last piece to this responsibility and accountability puzzle is this idea of problem solving and adaptability. When our teens know how to solve challenges and navigate setbacks, they are developing resilience, which is the key to responsibility and independence.

Two ways you can nurture your teen's problem solving and adaptability skills are by gradually increasing their responsibility and encouraging them to reflect. Let's look at each of these a bit more...

Gradually Increase Responsibility

If we want our teens to grow up and be responsible, independent adults, then we have to give them opportunities to put it into practice. That means providing them with opportunities to figure things out, to adapt, and to take on more over time.

By starting small and gradually adding more responsibilities over time, it helps teens build confidence and understand accountability in a more manageable way. This is especially important if your teen is younger, or if they have not had a lot of responsibility up to this point.

Here are age-appropriate suggestions for increasing responsibility for your teen:

Ages 10–12: Learning Basic Household Chores
- *To Start*: At this stage, kids can begin handling individual tasks like washing their own laundry, vacuuming their room, or emptying the dishwasher. This is a good time to introduce simple tasks and allow them to practice consistency.

- *Next Steps*: As they get comfortable, you can ask them to take on additional responsibilities like cleaning shared spaces (e.g., the living room), assisting with meal prep (e.g., chopping veggies or setting the table), and caring for pets.

Ages 13–16: Building Consistency and Accountability

- *To Start*: Teens can start taking on more complex responsibilities like doing all their laundry (from washing to folding), vacuuming the house, and taking out the trash. You can also introduce them to managing their own schedule, including keeping track of assignments, activities, and family obligations.

- *Next Steps*: Gradually add tasks like grocery shopping with a list, cooking a simple meal for the family, and managing a personal budget (e.g., their allowance). At this stage, they can start learning how to organize their time and balance multiple responsibilities.

Ages 17–19: Preparing for Independence

- *To Start*: By now, teens should manage more advanced tasks, such as taking care of their laundry without reminders, handling their own transportation (with a driving contract), and preparing full meals for the family. They should also manage personal finances, including saving for larger goals like a car or college.

- *Next Steps*: As they approach adulthood, encourage them to manage even more of their own responsibilities, such as scheduling appointments, paying for gas, or contributing to household bills. This is also the time to guide them through the process of finding a part-time job or internship and learning how to manage work alongside school.

By increasing responsibility step-by-step, teens develop the skills they'll need for living independently while gaining confidence and accountability along the way. You can help by offering guidance, setting expectations, and giving your teen more autonomy as they demonstrate readiness.

Self-Reflection

Not everyone is a natural problem solver or great at adapting. However, it is a skill your teen can nurture and develop. One of the easiest ways to help your teen develop this skill is by teaching the art of self-reflection.

Reflecting on personal decisions is key to problem solving. Self-reflection helps teens adapt and grow by evaluating past actions and strategizing for future challenges.

Accountability starts with recognizing mistakes and learning from them. Encourage your teen to reflect on their decisions. What went well? What could they improve? This helps them adapt to future challenges by learning from their experiences. Have them consider the following questions:

- What could I have done differently?

- How can I make sure this doesn't happen again?

- What did I learn from solving this problem that can help me in the future?

- What was one unexpected situation I faced recently, and how did I adapt to it?

- What's one situation where I resisted change, and how could I have handled it differently?

Learning how to reflect on our actions, our decisions, and even the situation or problem itself is going to help us grow and be more prepared for the curveballs that life often throws at us.

Personal responsibility and accountability are truly essential, foundational blocks to independence and lifelong success. The sooner we can help our teens learn these skills, the sooner they can be prepared for life after high school.

Conclusion

As we wrap up this chapter on independence, it's clear that personal responsibility and accountability are the cornerstones of raising self-sufficient teens. These skills are not only essential for managing daily tasks but also for navigating the bigger challenges in life. By teaching your teen to take ownership of their actions, to be accountable for their decisions, and to solve problems effectively, you are laying the groundwork for a successful transition into adulthood. This may be the final chapter of the book, but your journey with your teen doesn't stop here. Now that you've learned how to guide them in becoming independent, there are even more resources available to help you and your family continue to grow.

In the next chapter, we'll introduce you to the programs, tools, and community we've developed to support you as you raise teens who are ready to face the world confidently and competently. Remember, you don't have to do it alone—Adulting University is here to walk alongside you every step of the way. Together, let's empower the next generation to thrive.

Put It Into Practice

Here are some activities that you can do with your teen to practice the things we discussed in this chapter and help your teen be on their way to independence and self-sufficiency!

1. JOINT ACTIVITY: Develop an Independence Project

Work with your teen to select a project that they will manage from start to finish, such as planning a family outing, creating a weekly meal plan, or organizing a community service event. This activity will allow them to practice responsibility and accountability while you guide and support them along the way.

2. SEPARATE ACTIVITY: Start a Personal Accountability Journal

Have your teen start a daily journal where they record tasks they handle, how they felt about completing them, and areas for improvement. You, as the parent, can do the same for your own daily responsibilities. At the end of the week, compare journals and discuss lessons learned.

3. TOGETHER EXERCISE: Set Goals

Sit down with your teen and set both short-term and long-term goals. These could range from academic achievements to personal growth targets. Discuss the steps needed to reach these goals and how to stay accountable. This exercise helps reinforce the importance of planning, follow-through, and being accountable to oneself and others.

4. ROLE-PLAY: Practice Owning Up to Mistakes in Real Life

Role-play a scenario where your teen has made a mistake, such as missing a deadline or forgetting a commitment, and has to explain it to a parent, teacher, or boss. Practice how to take responsibility, acknowledge the mistake, and come up with a solution to prevent it from happening again. Then reverse roles and have your teen play the parent while you take on the role of the teen.

By putting these strategies into practice, you'll be able to guide your teen in mastering personal responsibility and accountability—skills that will serve them for a lifetime. And remember, if you're feeling overwhelmed or need more guidance, the resources in the next section will give you the support you need to keep going strong.

Your workbook is still waiting for you...

10

YOUR PARTNER IN PARENTING

ADDRESSING HOMESCHOOL FAMILIES' BIGGEST CHALLENGES

Congratulations on reaching this final chapter of *Adulting Unplugged*! You've taken a deep dive into the skills, mindsets, and guidance your teen needs to thrive. Now, I want you to take a deep breath. **Right now, you might be feeling one of two things:**

Overwhelmed. You just read through an entire book on teaching life skills, and you're wondering, *"How do I actually make all of this happen?"*

Doubtful. You might be thinking, *"Am I really doing enough? What if I miss something important? What if my teen isn't ready?"*

Maybe you're feeling **both.** And if that's the case, I want you to know: **You are not alone.** Every homeschool mom wrestles with these thoughts at some point.

But here's the good news—**you don't have to do this alone.**

Because while this book has given you **the foundation**, our program exists to **walk alongside you** so you don't have to figure it all out on your own.

The Reality of Raising Life-Ready Teens

Homeschooling is **incredible**, but let's be real—it can also feel **isolating.**

Maybe you're struggling with:

- A **teen who resists learning life skills**—and you don't want to fight them on it.

- Feeling **stretched thin** between homeschooling, running a business, and managing a household.

- Wondering if your teen is actually **learning what they need** to be independent.

- Feeling **alone** in the teen years and wishing for support from moms who *get it.*

These aren't just **random struggles**—they're the exact challenges I hear from homeschool moms **every single day.**

But what if you didn't have to **figure this all out on your own?**

What if instead of feeling **stressed, overwhelmed, and second-guessing yourself**—you had a community, a plan, and **real support** to help you **teach life skills in a way that works for your family?**

That's exactly why I created **Adulting University**.

How We Support You & Your Teen

At **Adulting University**, we provide **two ways** to help you navigate the journey of raising a capable, independent, life-ready teen.

OPTION 1: Level Up Your Life Mom's Inner Circle

Best for: Moms who want support, but whose kids may not be old enough yet or aren't ready for the full program.

Inside this group, you'll get:

- A **supportive community** of homeschool moms navigating the teen years.

- **Monthly coaching calls** to ask questions, get advice, and share wins.

- **Parent training & workshops** on topics like raising responsible teens, emotional intelligence, and career planning.

- **Access to our private resource library**, packed with trainings, tools, and templates to make teaching life skills easier.

You're already **doing so much**—homeschooling, running a business (or working), managing a household, and trying to make sure your teen is **actually ready** for the real world.

But let's be honest...

- You sometimes wonder if you're *missing something important*.

- You feel like you're *carrying the full weight* of preparing your teen alone.

- You wish you had a place to *ask questions, share wins, and learn from other moms*.

- You want a clear plan to teach these life skills without spending hours figuring it all out.

That's exactly why we created the **Level Up Mom's Inner Circle.**

Imagine This Instead...

- You wake up **feeling confident** that you're covering everything your teen needs.

- Instead of **feeling isolated**, you have **a supportive group of moms** navigating the same stage of life.

- You **stop second-guessing yourself** because you have **monthly coaching, expert workshops, and a proven roadmap.**

- You have **less stress** because you finally have **tools, strategies, and resources that make teaching life skills easy.**

This means:

- **More peace of mind** in your homeschool.

- **Less overwhelm** trying to piece everything together.

- **A stronger relationship with your teen** because you're guiding them with clarity instead of frustration.

And for your teen?

Even if they're **not ready to jump in just yet**, they **still benefit from everything you're learning**. You'll have:

- **A plan** to gradually introduce life skills in a way that **makes sense for them.**

- **A deeper understanding** of what they need—and **how to meet them where they are.**

- **A resource bank** of trainings & tools that you can use at any time.

This isn't just a **mom support group.** It's your **full how-to to raising independent, confident, capable young adults—without carrying all the weight alone.**

OPTION 2: Level Up Your Life All In

Best for: Moms who want **everything**—support for themselves + a **structured program for their teen.**

If you're ready for **next-level support**, this program gives you **the full package**:

- **Everything in the Homeschool Moms' Success Circle**—so you have **guidance & a community.**

- **Full access to our student program**—where your teen gets a **fully gamified, fun, but real world training.**

- **Engaging, interactive lessons**—so you're not the one having to teach it all.

- **Mentorship & guidance**—so your teen hears these lessons from someone *other than mom.*

- **Real-world skills training**—covering financial literacy, emotional intelligence, independence, and more.

This program **takes the weight off your shoulders** and **gives your teen the tools they need**—without the battles or pushback.

It's the **all-in experience** for families who are serious about preparing their teen for adulthood **the right way.**

Best for: Moms who want a **fully immersive life skills experience** for their teen—so they **learn, apply, and master** real-world skills while being part of a like-minded community.

If you've ever thought, **"I know my teen needs this, but I don't think they'll actually do it"**—you're not alone.

That's exactly why we created **Level Up Your Life—a gamified, interactive, and community-driven program** that makes learning life skills **engaging, motivating, and FUN for your teen**—while taking the pressure off YOU.

What This Looks Like for Your Teen

This isn't just another online course. **Your teen isn't sitting through boring lessons** or watching videos they'll never use.

Instead, they're stepping into a **fully immersive experience** where they:

- **Earn XP points, badges, and rewards** by leveling up their life skills.

- **Connect with other homeschool teens** in clubs, hangouts, and team challenges.

- **Go beyond the basics** by diving into deeper learning tracks like financial literacy, career readiness, or personal growth.

- **Build real-world confidence** through hands-on activities, mentorship, and leadership opportunities.

This program **meets them where they are** and **grows with them every year**—so they continue to develop new skills as they prepare for adulthood.

What They'll Learn (And Actually Apply!)

Every year, they'll **keep leveling up their skills** in things like:

- **Money Management** – Budgeting, saving, investing, and smart spending.

- **Communication & Relationships** – How to build meaningful friendships, resolve conflicts, and set boundaries.

- **Time Management & Productivity** – Learning to balance responsibilities, prioritize tasks, and manage their own schedule.

- **Career Exploration & Goal-Setting** – Discovering what they love and planning a path to success.

- **Independence & Responsibility** – From cooking and home management to decision-making and problem-solving.

- **Independence & Responsibility** – From cooking and home management to decision-making and problem-solving.

This isn't just another online course. **It's an interactive, hands-on experience.** Here's what makes **Level Up Your Life** different:

- **It's NOT just about learning—it's about DOING.** Every skill they unlock is something they practice, apply, and experience in real life.

- **They're part of a community.** They're learning alongside other teens their age, making friends, and motivating each other to keep growing.

- **Teens have the opportunity to go deeper**—with mentorship, additional courses, and leadership training for those who want to take it further.

The Transformation – What This Means for Your Family

For Your Teen:

- **They take ownership of their own learning**—without you nagging them.

- **They gain confidence** knowing they're developing real skills for adulthood.

- **They make friends & build relationships** with other motivated teens.

- **They feel excited** about learning life skills (seriously!).

For You (The Mom!):

- **You no longer have to do it all**—we're teaching these essential skills FOR YOU.

- **You stop worrying** whether your teen is ready for adulthood.

- **You get to focus on being their mom** instead of trying to be their life coach.

- **You watch them grow** into a responsible, capable, independent young adult.

The Choice is Yours — But You Don't Have to Do It Alone

The truth is, **reading this book is just the first step.** It is setting the foundation to build off of for your teen's future.

Now, you have two options:

OPTION 1: Do it all on your own—spending hours researching, planning, and piecemealing multiple curriculums and courses together. Hoping you're covering everything your teen needs.

OPTION 2: Let us help you. With a **clear plan, a community, and real support**, you don't have to figure it out alone.

Which one sounds easier?

If you're ready to **stop second-guessing yourself and start feeling confident** that you're giving your teen **exactly what they need**—I'd love to invite you to join us inside **Adulting University.**

Go to _https://adulting-university.com/levelup_ to learn more & find the right fit for your family.

I can't wait to support you in this journey!

Not Ready to Invest Yet? That's Okay!

We know every family's journey is unique, and we're here to support you, no matter where you're starting from. Check out our free and low-cost resources designed to provide guidance and insights that you can start using right away!

- **Facebook Group**—Join our **Adulting Unplugged Homeschool Mama Community** for ongoing support, tips, and discussions with other homeschool parents navigating the teen years.

- **Podcast**—Tune in to our podcast **<u>Adulting Unplugged: Unfiltered Real Talk on Parenting Teens & Young Adults</u>** for expert advice, parent stories, and actionable tips on preparing teens for life after high school.

- **Blog**—Dive into the **Adulting U Blog** for articles, tools, and insights to help you homeschool with confidence.

- **Partners & Resources**—Explore our carefully curated **<u>partner and resource page</u>**on our website, where you'll find trusted tools and additional support from organizations aligned with our mission.

Explore these resources and get a feel for how Adulting University can make a difference in your homeschool journey.

And if you want to talk to us to see what the best option is for your family, schedule a complimentary discovery call **HERE!**

ABOUT THE AUTHOR

Traci Bakenhaster is a passionate educator, coach, and advocate for teens, with over 13 years of experience empowering young people to thrive in adulthood. As the founder and CEO of **Adulting University**, Traci has worked with countless families to teach essential life skills, career exploration, and college readiness.

Traci holds a Master of Science in Business Psychology, a Bachelor of Science in Business Administration, and two associate degrees, reflecting her commitment to lifelong learning. She is certified in Youth Mental Health First Aid and as a Financial Coach, equipping her to guide teens through life's challenges with both compassion and expertise.

Throughout her career, Traci has served as a career coach, financial educator, and teen mentor, helping students navigate critical topics like personal responsibility, financial literacy, and mental health. She also collaborates with **Teen Wise**, supporting teen girls in building confidence and strong relationships.

But at her core, Traci is a proud homeschool mom. She and her husband of 6 years are raising and homeschooling their two kids—a preteen son and a toddler daughter—alongside their three fur babies: Bear, a Great Pyrenees, and two cats, Elsa and Figaro. Whether exploring new adventures with her kids or chasing after their pets, family is her "why" and the driving force behind everything she does.

Traci created *Adulting Unplugged* to support homeschool moms in raising self-sufficient, capable teens ready to face the real world. When she's not coaching, teaching, or mentoring, you can find her connecting with families in her thriving online community, creating resources that make life easier, or chasing after her own kids at home.

Learn more at **Adulting-University.com**.